Historical Analysis of Wetlands and Their Functions for the Nanticoke River Watershed. A Comparison between Pre-settlement and 1998 Conditions.

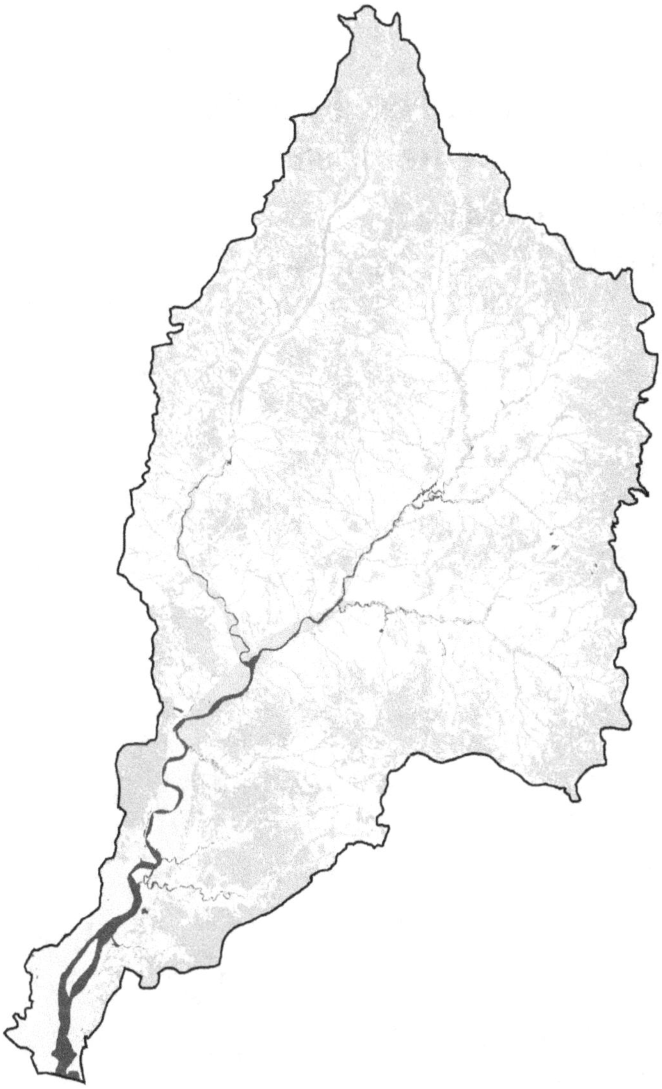

Pre-settlement 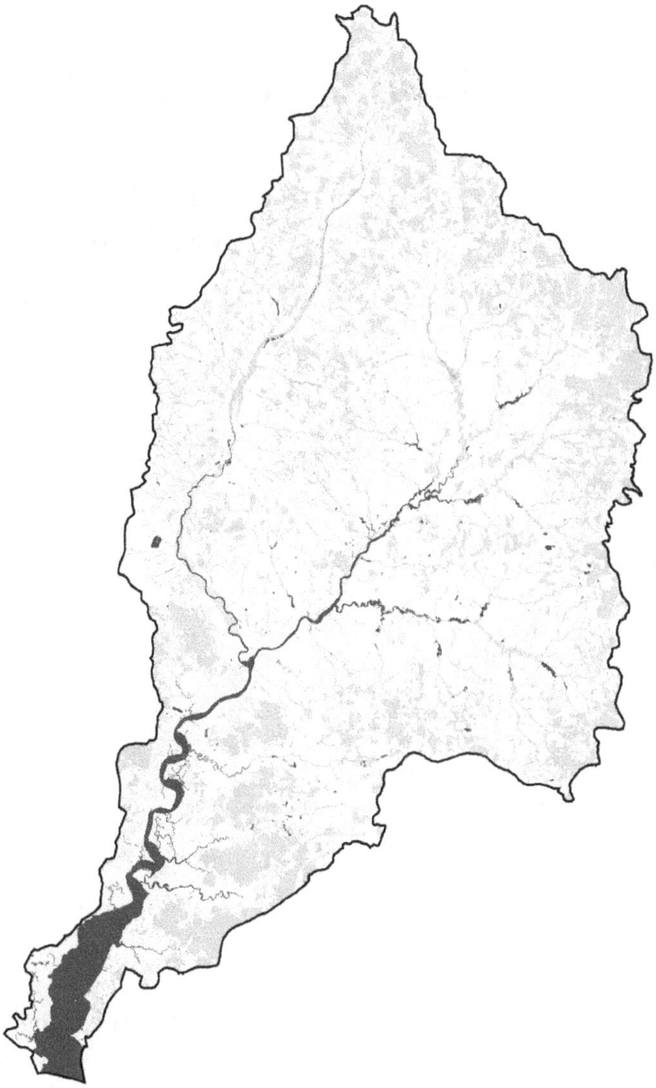   **1998**

National Wetlands Inventory   November 2003

Region 5

Historical Analysis of Wetlands and Their Functions For the Nanticoke River Watershed: A Comparison between Pre-settlement and 1998 Conditions

U.S. Fish and Wildlife Service
National Wetlands Inventory
Northeast Region
Hadley, MA 01035

November 2003

Historical Analysis of Wetlands and Their Functions for the Nanticoke River
Watershed: A Comparison between Pre-settlement and 1998 Conditions

by

R.W. Tiner and H.C. Bergquist

U.S. Fish and Wildlife Service
Northeast Region
National Wetlands Inventory Program
300 Westgate Center Drive
Hadley, MA 01035

Prepared for:
Kent Conservation District
3500 S. DuPont Highway
Dover, DE 19901

and

Maryland Eastern Shore Resource Conservation & Development Council
8133 Elliot Road, Suite 201
Easton, MD 21601-7131

November 2003

Table of Contents

Appendices

A.   Dichotomous Keys and Mapping Codes for Wetland Landscape Position, Landform, Water Flow Path, and Waterbody Type Descriptors (Tiner 2003a)

B.   Correlating Enhanced NWI Data with Wetland Functions for Watershed Assessments: A Rationale for Northeastern U.S. Wetlands (Tiner 2003b)

Thematic Maps in separate folder on the CD

Introduction

The states of Delaware and Maryland are cooperating to investigate and evaluate wetlands of the Nanticoke River watershed. They are collecting data on reference wetlands to gain information on wetland functions and levels of performance for evaluating impacts to presentday wetlands and to develop a watershed-based strategy for wetland conservation and restoration. The U.S. Fish and Wildlife Service is assisting the states in several ways. Roughly two years ago, the states provided funds to the U.S. Fish and Wildlife Service to expand the current National Wetlands Inventory (NWI) digital data to include hydrogeomorphic-type descriptors (i.e., landscape position, landform, and water flow path) to all mapped wetlands and to use these data to produce a preliminary assessment of wetland functions for the watershed. The results of this analysis were published in two watershed-based reports on the Nanticoke wetlands, one for Maryland and the other for Delaware (Tiner et al. 2000, 2001).

Upon receipt of this information, the states became interested in gaining a historical perspective on wetlands and the impact of estimated losses on wetland functions. In 2002 and 2003, funding was provided to the Service by the Kent Conservation District and Maryland Eastern Shore Resource Conservation & Development Council to design and conduct a historical assessment of wetlands in the Nanticoke River watershed.

Study Purpose

The purpose of the project was to produce a historical perspective of wetlands and their functions for the Nanticoke River watershed and compare these findings to previous work done for contemporary wetlands in this watershed. The specific objectives were: 1) to produce a map showing the general extent of wetlands prior to European colonization, 2) to use this information to prepare a preliminary functional assessment of pre-settlement wetlands, 3) to create a consistent database of contemporary wetlands for the entire watershed from existing enhanced NWI data, 4) to prepare a preliminary functional assessment for the watershed for contemporary wetlands, and 5) to compare the changes in wetland functions and extent based on the pre-settlement and contemporary wetland assessments. This information will assist wetland managers in wetland planning and evaluation at the watershed level. This report describes study methods and presents the results.

Organization of Report

The report is organized into the following sections: Study Area, Methods, General Scope and Limitations of the Study, Results, Discussion, Conclusions, Acknowledgments, and References. Two appendices provide keys to hydrogeomorphic wetland classification and the rationale for correlating wetland characteristics with wetland functions. Thematic maps are contained in a separate folder on the CD version of this report with linkages provided.

Study Area

The study area is the Nanticoke River watershed which begins in western Delaware and drains in a southwesterly direction into Maryland and ultimately into Chesapeake Bay (Figure 1). This watershed is roughly 800-square miles in size and includes about 25 percent of the state of Delaware. Major tributaries include five in Delaware (Broad Creek, Deep Creek, Gravelly Branch, Gum Branch, and Marshyhope Creek) and four in Maryland (Marshyhope Creek, Rewastico Creek, Quantico Creek, and Wetipquin Creek).

Figure 1. Locus map showing Nanticoke River watershed.

Methods

Pre-settlement Wetland Inventory

The distribution and extent of pre-settlement wetlands were determined from two sources: 1) soil survey data from the U.S.D.A. Natural Resource Conservation Service (NRCS) and the Delaware Department of Natural Resources and Environmental Control (DNREC) and 2) U.S. Geological Survey topographic maps. The former source was the primary source and most historic wetlands were identified from this material. The latter source was used to "lost" estuarine wetlands that are now open water.

Hydric soil map units from soil survey data were identified as historic wetlands. A digital database of hydric soil map units was created for the Nanticoke watershed from existing digital soil survey data and from soil map unit data in published soil surveys. Two counties had digital soils data available: Dorchester (SSURGO data from NRCS based on Brewer et al. 1998) and Sussex (from DNREC). For other counties (Caroline, Wicomico, and Kent), hydric soil digital data were created by scanning individual soil survey maps from county soil survey reports (Matthews 1964; Hall 1970; Matthews and Ireland 1971, respectively). Scanning was done at 300 dots per inch (dpi) and saved as TIFF images. The black color band (all linework) was selected in each image and copied to form a composite image (mosaic) for the county. Mosaics were georeferenced in ARCGIS 8.0 using the georeferencing extension, with a 1:24,000 digital raster graphics (DRG) serving as the base. These mosaics were then converted to georeferenced GRIDS and then to linear coverages which were converted to polygonal coverages and finally to shapes. The shapes were edited and hydric soil map units labeled using the georeferencing image to code ID in the background in ARCGIS 8.3.

Certain soil map units were identified as historic wetlands. These units were represented by hydric soil series or land types that are equated with wetlands (e.g., Swamp, Tidal Marsh, and Muck). Table 1 presents a list of the soil map units that were considered wetlands.

The soil-based historic wetland data were compared with existing NWI data to identify possible large wetland complexes (typically forested wetlands) that were not recorded as historic wetlands by soils data. When one overlays digital data sets derived from different sources and using different bases, there are usually many "slivers" that are detected due to problems matching the two data sets (i.e., alignment problems). By establishing a 12-acre threshold for identifying significant NWI omissions, the sliver issue was resolved. The remaining NWI wetlands not included in the hydric soil coverage were added to the historic data base. This process allowed for a more consistent comparison between wetland data for the two eras.

3

Table 1. Hydric soil series that were considered historic wetlands in the general study area. <u>Note</u>: Some of these soils may occur outside the Nanticoke River watershed.

Soil Series/Land Type	County
Bayboro	Caroline, Wicomico, and Kent
Beaches	Wicomico and Dorchester
Berryland	Sussex
Bestpitch and Transquaking	Dorchester
Bibb	Caroline
Chicone	Dorchester
Coastal Beach/Dune Land*	Sussex and Kent
Elkton	Caroline, Wicomico, Dorchester, Sussex, and Kent
Fallsington	Caroline, Wicomico, Dorchester, Sussex, and Kent
Fill Land	Sussex
Fluvaquents	Dorchester
Honga peat	Dorchester
Hurlock	Dorchester
Johnston	Caroline, Sussex, and Kent
Leon	Wicomico
Made Land	Caroline and Wicomico
Mixed Alluvial Land	Caroline, Wicomico, and Sussex
Muck	Caroline, Wicomico, and Sussex
Nanticoke	Dorchester
Osier	Sussex
Othello	Caroline, Wicomico, Dorchester, and Kent
Othello and Kentuck	Dorchester
Plummer	Caroline, Wicomico, and Sussex
Pocomoke	Caroline, Wicomico, Sussex, and Kent
Pone	Dorchester
Portsmouth	Caroline, Wicomico
Puckum	Dorchester
Rutlege	Wicomico and Sussex
St. Johns	Wicomico
Swamp	Caroline, Wicomico, Sussex, and Kent
Sunken	Dorchester
Tidal Marsh	Caroline, Wicomico, Sussex, and Kent

*Includes both wetland (beach) and upland (dune).

We recognized that over the past 500 years estuarine wetlands have migrated landward (upriver) and permanent inundation of low-lying estuarine marshes has occurred due to rising sea level. We therefore had to: 1) relocate the pre-settlement estuarine-riverine break further downriver than its current location and 2) add "lost" estuarine wetlands. For the former, we used the presence of soils recognized as submerged uplands and the appearance of salt-stressed forests to help establish this break at the mouth of the Baron Creek. Understandably, this is a conservative demarcation as it is likely that freshwater forested wetlands also occurred downstream along the edges of estuarine wetlands. The Honga and Sunken series (submerged "uplands," now brackish tidal wetlands) both represent former "uplands" (likely low-lying wet flatwoods similar to those growing today on Othello and Elkton soils) that became estuarine wetlands with rising sea level over the past few hundred years. The former soil is an organic soil (Terric Sulfihemists) with more than 16 inches of organic matter overlying mineral soil (Brewer et al. 1998). In contrast, the Sunken series is a mucky silt loam soil (Typic Ochraquults) with only 2-8 inches of organic matter forming a surface layer. This soil is typified by salt-stressed (dying or dead) stands of loblolly pine (Pinus taeda), while some areas have converted to salt/brackish marshes (Figure 2). While both series represent former "uplands," for purposes of this study, we identified only the Sunken series as a former freshwater forested wetlands that may have existed prior to European settlement. By the thickness of its organic horizon, the Honga series most likely represents former "upland" that became estuarine wetland longer than 300 years ago (e.g., wood found in the organic and mineral horizons was carbon-dated at less than 700 years before present; Brewer et al. 1998). Our interpretation is therefore conservative; others might consider all Honga soils to be freshwater wetland prior to settlement. For our study, the approximation used is satisfactory. Moreover, it is also possible that some areas of Othello and Elkton soils, for example, were upland soils (Mattapex, Mattapeake, or Keyport) at that time (Jim Brewer, pers. comm. 2003). Pone soils are drier than Puckham soils and were designated as temporarily flooded-tidal forested wetlands when they were contiguous with tidal marsh soils. In other places, they were designated as nontidal temporarily flooded forested wetlands. Muck soils (referenced in other soil surveys) and contiguous soils that are now classified as estuarine wetlands were also identified as historic tidal forested wetlands. Elsewhere, muck soil map units were regarded as nontidal forested wetlands. The Nanticoke series and the tidal marsh map units from the soil surveys were considered freshwater tidal marsh for the pre-settlement era. The pre-settlement limits of estuarine and freshwater tidal reaches therefore represent approximate boundaries (educated guess), mainly used to indicate a significant ecological and hydrological change in this watershed over time. We also recognized that the upstream limit of tidal influence was probably downstream from its current location, but lacked information to aid in redefining this limit.

To identify "lost" estuarine wetlands due to sea level rise over the past few hundred years, we referred to U.S. Geological Survey 1:24,000 topographic maps (Deal Island 1972, Mardela Springs 1982, Nanticoke 1983, and Wetipquin 1983) and located shallow water areas less than 6 feet (2 meters) deep (i.e., the shallowest depth recorded as a depth contour on the maps). These shallow water areas were predicted to be former estuarine wetlands (probably some combination of tidal marshes and flats) at some time prior to European colonization. Since the 6-foot (or 2m) depth was shown as a bottom contour line on the topographic maps, it served as a practical mark for identifying the lower boundary of pre-settlement intertidal wetlands for our study. Again, this is an approximate, not absolute, boundary.

Impounded sections of rivers (i.e., artificial in-stream ponds and lakes) shown on the soil surveys needed to be classified as some type of pre-settlement wetland. They were predicted to have been forested wetlands on hydric soils similar to contiguous wetlands above and below the impoundment. Some minor acreage of open water was probably included in the wetland acreage following this interpretation.

After pre-settlement wetlands were identified, they were classified according to NWI types (Cowardin et al. 1979; Table 2). We considered all inland wetlands to be palustrine forested wetlands[1], recognizing that periodic wildfires would have created a succession of types from emergent wetlands through shrub swamps to forested wetlands, much like we observe today after timber harvest. The condition of the historic landscape is therefore much simplified. We did not separate forested wetlands into different types at the subclass level according to Cowardin et al. (1979) since this was impossible to predict. Water regimes were assigned to pre-settlement wetlands based on descriptions of seasonal high water tables for individual hydric soils (soil map unit) from the published soil survey reports.

Figure 2. Area of Honga soil showing salt-stressed pines along marsh edge. (Brewer et al. 2003)

---

[1]According to the 1920s soil surveys, most of the soils were forested in their original state (e.g., Wicomico County was "practically" all forested until "reclaimed for agricultural purposes" - Snyder and Gillett 1925).

Table 2. Hydric soil map unit acreage for the Nanticoke River watershed and expected NWI type. Note: The total hydric soil acreage is less than the estimated pre-settlement wetland acreage because palustrine forested wetlands occurring on nonhydric soil map units were added; also dammed rivers and impoundments ("water") were classified as a vegetated wetland type equivalent to that predicted for adjacent hydric soil map units.

Soil Series/Land Type	Acreage	% of Total	Predicted NWI Type
Bayboro	145.3	<1	PFO_E
Beaches*	157.6	<1	E2EM, PFO_E
Berryland	108.9	<1	PFO_E
Bestpitch	3,100.0	1.4	E2EM
Chicone	313.3	<1	PFO_E, PFO_R
Elkton	6,186.8	2.9	PFO_A
Fallsington	102,356.3	47.7	PFO_A, PFO_S
Fill Land	60.2	<1	PFO_A, PFO_S
Fluvaquents	1,095.8	<1	PFO_E, PFO_R
Honga peat	4,671.1	2.2	E2EM
Hurlock	5,490.0	2.6	PEM_R, PFO_E, PFO_R
Johnston	11,200.8	5.2	PFO_E, PFO_R
Kentuck	761.2	<1	PFO_A
Leon	280.7	<1	PFO_A
Made Land	46.1	<1	E2EM, PEM_R, PFO_E
Mixed Alluvial Land	1,542.1	<1	PEMR, PFO_E, PFO_S, PFO_A
Muck	1,572.1	<1	E2EM, PFO_E, PFO_R
Nanticoke	998.6	<1	PEM_R, PFO_E
Osier	2,984.1	1.4	PFO_A, PFO_S
Othello	10,565.4	4.9	PFO_A
Plummer	3,338.4	1.6	PFO_A, PFO_S
Pocomoke	36,988.3	17.3	PFO_E, PFO_R
Pone	3,464.6	1.6	PFO_E, PFO_S
Portsmouth	682.5	<1	PFO_E
Puckum	4,196.6	2.0	PFO_E, PFO_R
Rutlege	1,747.2	<1	E2EM, PFO_E, PFO_R
St. Johns	65.2	<1	PFO_E
Sunken	675.0	<1	E2EM
Swamp	1,266.5	<1	PFO_E, PFO_R
Tidal Marsh	8,312.2	3.9	E2EM, PEM_R, PEM_F, PFO_E, PFO_R
------------------------	-------------		
Total	214,372.9		

*Beaches on the soil survey report were actually vegetated wetlands.

1998 Wetland Inventory

The foundation of this project was a fairly comprehensive, geospatial wetland database created by the Service's NWI Program. Basic NWI data included both geospatial data from standard NWI maps with wetlands classified according to Cowardin et al. (1979). NWI data for the Nanticoke watershed were recently updated using spring 1998-1:40,000 black and white photography (see Tiner et al. 2001, 2000 for details).

Enhanced Wetland Classification

Through our previous work (Tiner et al. 2001, 2000), the NWI database was expanded to include hydrogeomorphic-type properties for mapped wetlands. Landscape position, landform, water flow path, and waterbody types (LLWW descriptors) were applied to all wetlands in the NWI digital database by merging NWI data with on-line U.S. Geological Survey topographic maps (digital raster graphics) and consulting aerial photography where necessary (see Tiner et al. 2001, 2000). Appendix A of this report contains dichotomous keys for applying these descriptors. Previous work was reviewed and revised based on these keys.

Landscape position defines the relationship between a wetland and an adjacent waterbody, if present. Four landscape positions are relevant to the Nanticoke watershed: 1) lotic - along freshwater rivers and streams and periodically flooded at least during high discharge periods, 2) lentic - in lakes, reservoirs, and their basins with water levels significantly affected by the presence of these waterbodies, 3) terrene - isolated or headwater wetlands, fragments of former isolated or headwater wetlands that are now connected to downslope wetlands via drainage ditches, and wetlands on broad, flat terrain cut through by stream but where overbank flooding does not occur, and 4) estuarine - associated with tidal brackish waters (estuaries). Lotic wetlands are further separated by river and stream sections (based on watercourse width - polygon = river vs. linear = stream at a scale of 1:24,000) and then divided into one of five gradients: 1) high (e.g., shallow mountain streams on steep slopes - not present in the study areas), 2) middle (e.g., streams with moderate slopes - not present in the study areas), 3) low (e.g., mainstem rivers with considerable floodplain development and slow-moving streams), 4) intermittent (i.e., periodic flows), and 5) tidal (i.e., under the influence of the tides).

Landform is the physical form of a wetland or the predominant land mass on which it occurs (e.g., floodplain or interfluve). Six types are recognized in the Nanticoke watershed: basin, interfluve, flat, floodplain, fringe, and island (see Table 3 for definitions); no slope wetlands were identified due to the flat terrain of the coastal plain.

Additional modifiers were assigned to indicate water flow paths associated with wetlands: bidirectional, throughflow, inflow, outflow, or isolated. Surface water connections are emphasized because they are more readily identified than groundwater linkages. Bidirectional flow is two-way flow either related to tidal influence (bidirectional-tidal) or water level fluctuations in lakes and impoundments (bidirectional-nontidal). Throughflow wetlands have either a watercourse or another type of wetland above and below them, so water flows through these wetlands. All lotic wetlands are throughflow types. Inflow wetlands are sinks where no surface water outlets exist, yet water is entering via a stream or river (often intermittent) or an

Table 3. Definitions and examples of landform types (Tiner 2003a). Map codes in parentheses.

Landform Type	General Definition	Examples
Basin* (BA)	a depressional (concave) landform (including tidal wetlands with restricted flow)	lakefill bogs; wetlands in the saddle between two hills; wetlands in closed or open depressions, including narrow stream valleys; tidal marshes with restricted flow
Slope (SL)	a landform extending uphill (on a slope)	seepage wetlands on hillsides; wetlands along drainageways or mountain streams on slopes
Flat* (FL)	a relatively level landform, often on broad level landscapes	wetlands on flat areas with high seasonal ground-water levels; wetlands on terraces along rivers/streams; wetlands on hillside benches; wetlands at toes of slopes
Floodplain (FP)	a broad, generally flat landform occurring on a landscape shaped by fluvial or riverine processes	wetlands on alluvium; bottomland swamps
Interfluve (IF)	a broad, level to imperceptibly depressional poorly drained landform occurring between two drainage systems (i.e., on interstream divides)	flatwood wetlands on coastal or glaciolacustrine plains
Fringe (FR)	a landform occurring within the banks of a river or stream or along the shores of a waterbody (estuary, river, stream, pond, lake, or ocean) that is either: vegetated and semipermanently flooded or wetter, or permanently saturated due to this location, or irregularly flooded (tidal wetlands with unrestricted flow) or a nonvegetated bank or shore that is seasonally flooded or temporarily flooded	buttonbush swamps; aquatic beds; salt and brackish marshes with unrestricted tidal flow; cobble-gravel beds and bars in and along streams
Island (IL)	a landform completely surrounded by water (including deltas)	deltaic and insular wetlands; floating bog islands

*May be applied as sub-landforms within the Interfluve (IFba, IFfl) and Floodplain (FPba, FPfl).

9

upslope wetland. Outflow wetlands have water leaving them and moving downstream via a watercourse or a slope wetland; they are often sources of streams. Isolated wetlands are essentially closed ("geographically isolated") depressions or flats where water comes from direct precipitation, localized surface water runoff, and/or ground water discharge. From the surface water perspective, these wetlands are "isolated" from other wetlands since they lack an apparent surface water connection, however it must be recognized that they may be hydrologically linked to other wetlands and waterbodies via groundwater.

Other descriptors applied to mapped wetlands include headwater, drainage-divide, fragmented, partly drained, human-induced outflow, and human-impacted. Headwater wetlands are sources of streams or wetlands along first-order (perennial) streams. They include wetlands connected to first-order streams by ditches; they were labeled with a partly drained modifier as were other wetlands with ditches draining them. Many such wetlands are remnants of once larger interfluve wetlands that naturally drained into streams. A complex of such remnants when in close proximity to one another was typically treated as a single unit for water flow path classification purposes. Wetlands occurring in more than one watershed or subbasin or straddling the defined watershed boundary line between a watershed or subbasin and a neighboring one, were classified as drainage-divide wetlands. We identified pieces of wetlands separated by major highways (federal and state roads) as fragmented wetlands. This is a first step in addressing the issue of fragmentation which is quite complex and beyond the scope of our work. For example, we did not apply the descriptor to wetlands that were simply reduced in size due to land use practices. The listing of fragmented wetlands is therefore extremely conservative. Human-induced outflow wetlands were identified in the Delaware portion of the watershed only based on previous work. They are wetlands where outflow is now through the drainage ditch network. Human-impacted wetlands are those significantly altered by excavation or impoundment.

For open water habitats such as the ocean, estuaries, lakes, and ponds, additional descriptors following Tiner (2003a) were applied.

Note: There may be minor discrepancies between the 1998 classification and the historic wetland classification due to source data and how the datasets were compiled. The former is more detailed than the latter as more lotic stream wetlands were identified. These wetlands are the remnants of once larger wetlands (identified as terrene interfluve types) that have been essentially reduced in size to follow the narrow stream. These wetlands might have always been lotic stream wetlands but fell within large wetland complexes (hydric soil mapping unit) characterized as terrene interfluve wetlands.

Preliminary Assessment of Wetland Functions

After improving and enhancing the NWI digital database, analyses were performed to produce a preliminary assessment of wetland functions for the watershed. Ten wetland functions were evaluated: 1) surface water detention, 2) streamflow maintenance, 3) nutrient transformation, 4) sediment and other particulate retention, 5) coastal storm surge detention, 6) shoreline stabilization, 7) provision of fish and shellfish habitat, 8) provision of waterfowl and waterbird habitat, 9) provision of other wildlife habitat, and 10) conservation of biodiversity. The latter function was not evaluated for the pre-settlement era since source data were limited.

This study employed a watershed assessment approach that may be called "Watershed-based Preliminary Assessment of Wetland Functions" (W-PAWF). W-PAWF applies general knowledge about wetlands and their functions to develop a watershed overview that highlights possible wetlands of significance in terms of performance of various functions. The rationale for correlating wetland characteristics with wetland functions is described in a separate report included as Appendix B (Tiner 2003b).

After running the analyses, a series of maps for watershed were generated to highlight wetland types that may perform these functions at high or other significant levels. Statistics (acreage summaries) were generated from Microsoft's Access program, whereas topical maps were generated by ArcView software. (Note: Recompilation of statistics from the database may produce slightly different acreage totals than reported herein due to format conversions and computer round-off procedures. Any difference should be minor, amounting to less than 1% of the reported value.)

Extent of Natural Habitat

Maps showing the extent of natural habitat in the Nanticoke watershed were prepared. The pre-settlement map was based largely on interpretation of soil map units, while the 1998 map came from previous work in the watershed (Tiner et al. 2001, 2000).

Function Comparison: Pre-settlement vs. 1998

To assess the cumulative loss of wetlands on specific functions, one can simply examine the change in acreage of specific wetland types. This was done, but the acreage difference alone may not adequately convey the cumulative impact of the lost acreage on wetland function. To address the latter, the senior author devised a simple weighting scale for wetlands of potential significance for each function. A "high" potential was given a weight of 2, while a "moderate" potential and other significant wetlands were assigned a weight of 1. By multiplying the wetland acreage listed as high, moderate, or other potential by the weighting factor, a total number of functional units was calculated for each function at pre-settlement and 1998. This would allow comparison between pre-settlement functional capacity (total functional units for time one) and the 1998 capacity (total functional units for time two) and could demonstrate a percent loss of pre-settlement function. This provides an interesting perspective on the current conditions from a functional capacity standpoint and perhaps gives a better sense of the relative magnitude of the functional loss than wetland acreage loss alone.

General Scope and Limitations of the Study

Pre-settlement Wetland Inventory

Historic wetland data compiled from contemporary soil surveys produced the most accurate depiction of pre-settlement wetlands for the Nanticoke River watershed prepared to date. Translating this information to historic wetland extent required making certain assumptions: 1) hydric soil mapping units represent historic wetlands, 2) areas of the Sunken series were freshwater forested wetlands at pre-settlement, 3) areas of typical freshwater wetland soils that are now mapped as estuarine wetlands were also freshwater forested wetlands at pre-settlement, 4) areas of Honga series were estuarine wetlands at this time, although they were forested wetlands at least 700 years ago (Brewer et al. 1998), and 5) areas within nonhydric soil map units that were mapped as forested wetlands in 1998 were forested wetlands at pre-settlement.

1998 Wetland Inventory and Digital Database

Despite being five years "old," the 1998 database should reasonably reflect contemporary conditions. One must, however, recognize the limitations of any wetland mapping effort derived mainly through photointerpretation techniques (see Tiner 1997, 1999 for details). For example, use of spring aerial photography for wetland mapping precludes identification of freshwater aquatic beds. Such areas are included within areas mapped as open water (e.g., lacustrine and palustrine unconsolidated bottom) because vegetation is not developed so they appear as water on the aerial photographs. Also drier-end wetlands such as seasonally saturated and temporarily flooded palustrine wetlands are often difficult to separate from nonwetlands through photointerpretation.

Preliminary Assessment of Wetland Functions

At the outset, it is important to emphasize that this functional assessment is a preliminary one based on wetland characteristics interpreted through remote sensing and using the best professional judgment of the senior author and other wetland specialists (including specialists working in the Nanticoke River watershed). Wetlands believed to be providing potentially high or other significant levels of performance for a particular function were highlighted. As the focus of this report is on wetlands, an assessment of deepwater habitats (e.g., lakes, rivers, and estuaries) and linear features such as perennial and intermittent streams for providing the listed functions was not done. The importance of permanently flooded habitats to fish, for example, should be obvious and the beneficial functions of small streams (even intermittent ones) to water quality and sediment retention should also be recognized (Meyer et al. 2003). Also, no attempt was made to produce a more qualitative ranking for each function or for each wetland based on multiple functions as this would require more input from others and more data, well beyond the scope of this study. For a technical review of wetland functions, see Mitsch and Gosselink (2000) and for a broad overview, see Tiner (1985; 1998) and Tiner and Burke (1995).

Functional assessment of wetlands can involve many parameters. Typically such assessments have been done in the field on a case-by-case basis, considering observed features relative to those required to perform certain functions or by actual measurement of performance. The present study does not seek to replace the need for such evaluations as they are the ultimate assessment of the functions for individual wetlands. Yet, for a watershed analysis, basin-wide field-based assessments are not practical or cost-effective or even possible given access considerations. For watershed planning purposes, a more generalized assessment is worthwhile for targeting wetlands that may provide certain functions, especially for those functions dependent on landscape position, landform, vegetation life form, and other photointerpretable features. Subsequently, these results can be field-verified when it comes to actually evaluating particular wetlands for acquisition purposes, e.g., for conservation of biodiversity or for preserving flood storage capacity. Current aerial photography may also be examined to aid in further evaluations (e.g., condition of wetland/stream buffers or adjacent land use) that can supplement this preliminary assessment.

This study employs a watershed assessment approach that may be called "Watershed-based Preliminary Assessment of Wetland Functions" (W-PAWF). W-PAWF applies general knowledge about wetlands and their functions to develop a watershed overview that highlights possible wetlands of significance in terms of performance of various functions. To accomplish this objective, the relationships between wetlands and various functions must be simplified into a set of practical criteria or observable characteristics. Such assessments could also be further expanded to consider the condition of the associated waterbody and the neighboring upland or to evaluate the opportunity a wetland has to perform a particular function or service to society, for example.

W-PAWF usually does not account for the opportunity that a wetland has to provide a function resulting from a certain land-use practice upstream or the presence of certain structures or land-uses downstream. For example, two wetlands of equal size and like vegetation may be in the right landscape position to retain sediments. One, however, may be downstream of a land-clearing operation that has generated considerable suspended sediments in the water column, while the other is downstream from an undisturbed forest. The former should be actively performing sediment trapping in a major way, while the latter is not. Yet if land-clearing takes place upstream of the latter area, the second wetland will likely trap sediments as well as the first wetland. The entire analysis typically tends to ignore opportunity since such opportunity may have occurred in the past or may occur in the future and the wetland is awaiting a call to perform this service at higher levels than presently.

W-PAWF also does not consider the condition of the adjacent upland (e.g., level of disturbance) or the actual water quality of the associated waterbody which may be regarded as important metrics for assessing the health of individual wetlands (not part of this study). Collection and analysis of these data were done as another part of prior studies (Tiner et al. 2000, 2001) and were not part of the present study.

We further emphasize that the preliminary assessment does not obviate the need for more detailed assessments of the various functions. This assessment should be viewed as a starting point for more rigorous assessments, as it attempts to cull out wetlands that may likely provide significant functions based on generally accepted principles and the source information used for this analysis. This type of assessment is most useful for regional or watershed planning purposes. For site-specific evaluations, additional work will be required, especially field verification and collection of site-specific data for potential functions (e.g., following the HGM assessment approach as described by Brinson 1993 and other onsite evaluation procedures). This is particularly true for assessments of fish and wildlife habitats and biodiversity. Other sources of data may exist to help refine some of the findings of this report. Additional modeling could be done, for example, to identify habitats of likely significance to individual species of animals (based on their specific life history requirements).

Field checking of seasonally flooded and seasonally flooded/saturated emergent wetlands should be done to determine if they are marshes or wet meadows. If the former, they will likely have high potential as both fish and shellfish habitat and waterfowl habitat rather than the moderate rating given in this report.

Rationale for Preliminary Functional Assessments

Correlations were established between wetland characteristics in the wetland database and ten functions: 1) surface water detention, 2) streamflow maintenance, 3) nutrient transformation, 4) sediment and other particulate retention, 5) coastal storm surge detention, 6) shoreline stabilization, 7) provision of fish and wildlife habitat, 8) provision of waterfowl and waterbird habitat, 9) provision of other wildlife habitat, and 10) conservation of biodiversity. These correlations were based on a general review of the scientific literature and professional judgment of the senior author and other wetland specialists throughout the Northeast. The rationale for these correlations are presented in a separate report "Correlating Enhanced National Wetlands Inventory Data with Wetland Functions for Watershed Assessments: A Rationale for Northeastern U.S. Wetlands" (Tiner 2003b) which is included as Appendix B of this report.

The conservation of biodiversity function was only evaluated for the 1998 period. In the context of this report, the term "biodiversity" is used to identify certain wetland types that appear to be scarce or relatively uncommon in the watershed, or complexes of large wetlands. Schroeder (1996) noted that to conserve regional biodiversity, maintenance of large-area habitats for forest interior birds is essential. Robbins et al. (1989) suggested a minimum forest size of 7,410 acres to retain all species of the forest-breeding avifauna in the Mid-Atlantic region. For the Nanticoke watershed, we attempted to highlight uncommon wetlands, wetlands of potential high diversity, and areas that may be important for forest-breeding birds in the Mid-Atlantic region (i.e., forested areas 7,410 acres and larger containing contiguous palustrine forested wetlands and upland forests). All riverine tidal wetlands, palustrine tidal emergent wetlands, and oligohaline wetlands were identified as significant for this function because they are often colonized by a diverse assemblage of plants and are among the most diverse plant communities in the Mid-Atlantic region. Other wetlands deemed important for this function included Atlantic white cedar swamps and bald cypress swamps. We also identified wetlands that were uncommon types based on mapping classification (not on Natural Heritage Program data) including palustrine tidal evergreen forested wetlands, palustrine tidal scrub-shrub wetlands, and palustrine seasonally flooded and wetter emergent wetlands.

Use of Natural Heritage Program data and GAP data has been suggested, but these data were not provided for our use and to incorporate such data is beyond the scope of W-PAWF. It is expected that such information will be utilized at a later date by state agencies and others for more detailed planning and evaluation. The wetlands designated as potentially significant for biodiversity are simply a foundation to build upon. Local knowledge of significant wetlands will further refine the list of wetlands important for this function. For information on rare and endangered species, contact the Natural Heritage Program office.

Appropriate Use of this Report

The report provides a basic characterization of wetlands in the Nanticoke watershed including a preliminary assessment of wetland functions and historic changes since pre-colonial times. Keeping in mind the limitations mentioned above, the results are a first-cut or initial screening of the watershed's wetlands to designate wetlands that may have a significant potential to perform different functions. The targeted wetlands have been predicted to perform a given function at a significant level presumably important to the watershed's ability to provide that function. "Significance" is a relative term and is used in this analysis to identify wetlands that are likely to perform a given function at a level above that of wetlands not designated. Review of these preliminary findings and consideration of additional information not available to us may identify the need to modify some of the criteria used to identify wetlands of potential significance for certain functions.

While the results are useful for gaining an overall perspective of the watershed's wetlands and their relative importance in performing certain functions, the report does not identify differences among wetlands of similar type and function. The latter information is often critical for making decisions about wetland acquisition and designating certain wetlands as more important for preservation versus others with the same categorization. Additional information may be gained through consulting with agencies having specific expertise in a subject area and by conducting field investigations to verify the preliminary assessments. When it comes to actually acquiring wetlands for preservation, other factors must be considered. Such factors may include: 1) the condition of the surrounding area, 2) the ownership of the surrounding area and the wetland itself, 3) site-specific assessment of wetland characteristics and functions, 4) more detailed comparison with similar wetlands based on field data, and 5) advice from other agencies (federal, state, and local) with special expertise on priority resources (e.g., for wildlife habitat, contact appropriate federal and state biologists). The latter agencies may have site-specific information or field-based assessment methods that can aid in further narrowing the choices to help insure that the best wetlands are acquired for the desired purpose.

The report is a watershed-based wetland characterization for the Nanticoke watershed and a historical assessment of changes in wetland extent and function. The report does not make comparisons with other watersheds.

The report is useful for natural resource planning as an initial screening for considering prioritization of wetlands (for acquisition, restoration, or strengthened protection), as an educational tool (e.g., helping people better understand wetland functions and the relationships between wetland characteristics and performance of individual functions), for characterizing the differences among wetlands (both form and function), and for gaining perspective on how wetlands in the watershed have changed over time and how this has affected wetland functions.

Results

The wetland database created for this project allowed production of wetland maps and statistics on wetland extent and predicted functions for two time periods (pre-settlement and 1998). Study findings are presented in four subsections. The first subsection contains a list of the maps prepared for this project, while the next two subsections present the acreage summary findings for each era. The last subsection of the Results contains a comparative analysis of changes in wetland conditions and functions from pre-settlement to 1998. The report and accompanying maps may be posted on the NWI homepage (http://wetlands.fws.gov) under "reports and publications" in the near future.

Maps

Due to their size, the maps are included in a separate file on the compact disk (CD) containing this report. Two sets of maps were produced at a scale of 1:110,000 to profile the Nanticoke's wetlands - one set showing estimated pre-settlement conditions and predicted wetlands of significance for nine functions (excluding conservation of biodiversity) and the other set showing 1998 conditions and predicted wetlands of significance for ten functions.

A list of the maps follows:

<u>Pre-settlement Maps</u>

Map 1NW pre-settlement - Wetlands and Deepwater Habitats Classified by NWI Types
Map 2NW pre-settlement- Wetlands Classified by Landscape Position
Map 3NW pre-settlement - Wetlands Classified by Landform
Map 4NW pre-settlement - Wetlands Classified by Water Flow Path
Map 5NW pre-settlement - Potential Wetlands of Significance for Surface Water Detention
Map 6NW pre-settlement - Potential Wetlands of Significance for Streamflow Maintenance
Map 7NW pre-settlement - Potential Wetlands of Significance for Nutrient Transformation
Map 8NW pre-settlement - Potential Wetlands of Significance for Sediment and Other
  Particulate Retention
Map 9NW pre-settlement - Potential Wetlands of Significance for Coastal Storm Surge
  Detention
Map 10NW pre-settlement - Potential Wetlands of Significance for Shoreline Stabilization
Map 11NW pre-settlement - Potential Wetlands of Significance for Fish and Shellfish Habitat
Map 12NW pre-settlement - Potential Wetlands of Significance for Waterfowl and Waterbird
  Habitat
Map 13NW pre-settlement - Potential Wetlands of Significance for Other Wildlife Habitat
Map 14NW pre-settlement - Extent of Natural Habitat in the Nanticoke Watershed

<u>1998 Maps</u>

Map 1NW 1998 - Wetlands and Deepwater Habitats Classified by NWI Types
Map 2NW 1998 - Wetlands Classified by Landscape Position
Map 3NW 1998 - Wetlands Classified by Landform

Map 4NW 1998 - Wetlands Classified by Water Flow Path
Map 5NW 1998 - Potential Wetlands of Significance for Surface Water Detention
Map 6NW 1998 - Potential Wetlands of Significance for Streamflow Maintenance
Map 7NW 1998 - Potential Wetlands of Significance for Nutrient Transformation
Map 8NW 1998 - Potential Wetlands of Significance for Sediment and Other Particulate
  Retention
Map 9NW 1998 - Potential Wetlands of Significance for Coastal Storm Surge Detention
Map 10NW 1998 - Potential Wetlands of Significance for Shoreline Stabilization
Map 11NW 1998 - Potential Wetlands of Significance for Fish and Shellfish Habitat
Map 12NW 1998 - Potential Wetlands of Significance for Waterfowl and Waterbird Habitat
Map 13NW 1998 - Potential Wetlands of Significance for Other Wildlife Habitat
Map 14NW 1998 - Potential Wetlands of Significance for Biodiversity
Map 15NW 1998 - Extent of Natural Habitat in the Nanticoke Watershed

Pre-settlement Conditions

Historic wetlands were classified according to the U.S. Fish and Wildlife Service's official
wetland classification system (Cowardin et al. 1979) and by landscape position, landform, and
water flow path descriptors following Tiner (2003a). Wetland acreage summaries for the
Nanticoke watershed are given in Tables 4 and 5 and wetland distribution illustrated on Pre-
settlement Maps 1NW through 4NW. Table 4 summarizes acreage of wetland types through the
subclass level of the Service's classification ("NWI types"), while Table 5 tabulates statistical
data on wetlands by landscape position, landform, and water flow path ("LLWW types").

Wetlands by NWI Types

The predicted acreage of Nanticoke wetlands at pre-settlement was roughly 230,000 acres (Table
4) which represented about 45 percent of the watershed. The distribution of these wetlands by
major type is shown on Map 1NW pre-settlement.

Most (88.5%) of the wetlands were forested, with the rest being listed as emergent (10.3% as
estuarine and 1.2% as palustrine). Wild fires or fires set by Native Americans probably had a
substantial impact on plant composition of wetlands. The actual acreage of palustrine emergent
wetlands was undoubtedly greater than our estimate, but we had no reasonable means to predict
this effect. We also realize that these changes would be quite dynamic over time (related to fire
frequency and intensity). Our estimates also do not include acreage for palustrine scrub-shrub
wetlands, yet it is also likely that these successional communities were also present due to fire
impacts. There was no reasonable way to estimate their extent and distribution.

Table 4. Pre-settlement wetland acreage based on interpretation on soil survey data and U.S.G.S. topographic maps. <u>Note</u>: Totals may not sum exactly due to computer round-off.

Wetland Type	Acreage	% of Total Acreage
Estuarine Emergent*	23,636.8	10.3
Palustrine Emergent		
Seasonally Flooded-Tidal	2,696.5	1.2
Semipermanently Flooded	63.5	<0.1
Total	*2,760.0*	*1.2*
Palustrine Forested		
Seasonally Flooded-Tidal	6,459.1	2.8
Temporarily Flooded-Tidal	769.2	<0.1
Seasonally Flooded	63,498.1	27.6
Temporarily Flooded	132,896.1	57.8
Total	*203,622.5*	*88.5*
GRAND TOTAL	230,019.3	

*Includes an undetermined amount of estuarine unconsolidated shore (tidal flat).

Wetlands by LLWW Types

Prior to European settlement, the Nanticoke watershed had an estimated 2,809 wetlands occupying about 230,000 acres (Table 5). Seventy-eight percent of the acreage was terrene (e.g., wetlands at the head of the watershed or isolated forms) (Map 2NW pre-settlement). Wetlands associated with rivers and streams (lotic) accounted for about 12 percent of the acreage, while the remaining 10 percent was in the estuary. From the landform perspective, almost 77 percent of the acreage was represented by interfluve types occupying broad flat interstream divides between streams and other watersheds (Map 3NW pre-settlement). Most of the remaining acreage was either floodplain (10.4%) or fringe (11.2%). Nearly three-quarters (73.0%; 168,042.4 acres) of the acreage experienced outflow. Bidirectional-tidal flow affected 14.6 percent of the acreage (33,561.6 acres), while throughflow and geographically isolated acreage accounted for 7.4 percent (17,013.2 acres) and 5.0 percent (11,401.9 acres), respectively (Map 4NW pre-settlement).

Table 5. Pre-settlement wetland acreage classified by landscape position, landform, and water flow path. <u>Note</u>: Some totals may differ slightly due to round-off procedures; number of wetlands is approximate due to GIS processing.

Landscape Position	Landform	Water Flow Path	Approx. # of Wetlands	Pre-settlemt Acreage (% of Grand Total)	
Estuarine	Fringe	Bidirectional-tidal	83	22,793.6	(10.0)
	Island	Bidirectional-tidal	1	843.1	(0.3)
	Total		*84*	*23,636.7*	*(10.3)*
Lotic River	Floodplain	Bidirectional-tidal	102	7,181.0	(3.1)
		Throughflow	10	164.2	(<0.1)
		Subtotal	*112*	*7,345.2*	*(3.2)*
	Fringe	Bidirectional-tidal	105	2,696.5	(1.2)
		Throughflow	2	63.5	(<0.1)
		Subtotal	*107*	*2,760.0*	*(1.2)*
	Total		*219*	*10,105.2*	*(4.4)*
Lotic Stream	Floodplain	Bidirectional-tidal	2	47.3	(<0.1)
		Throughflow	130	16,476.5	(7.2)
		Subtotal	*132*	*16,523.8*	*(7.2)*
	Basin	Throughflow	12	73.2	(<0.1)
	Flat	Throughflow	13	168.5	(<0.1)
	Total		*157*	*16,765.5*	*(7.3)*
Terrene	Interfluve	Isolated	1723	11,401.9	(5.0)
		Outflow	380	164,638.7	(71.6)
		Throughflow	5	67.3	(<0.1)
		Subtotal	*2,108*	*176,107.9*	*(76.6)*
	Basin	Outflow	79	815.6	(0.4)
	Flat	Outflow	162	2,588.2	(1.1)
	Total		*2,349*	*179,511.7*	*(78.0)*
GRAND TOTAL			2,809	230,019.1	

Preliminary Functional Assessment

Most of the historic wetlands were predicted to perform four functions at significant levels: surface water detention (97.9% of all wetlands), streamflow maintenance (79.0%), nutrient transformation (100%), and provision of other wildlife habitat (100%) (Table 6). A significant level of sediment and other particulate retention was projected for nearly 44 percent of the wetlands. Other functions were estimated to be performed at significant levels by less than 25 percent of the wetlands: shoreline stabilization (22.0%), coastal storm surge detention (14.6%), provision of fish and shellfish habitat (18.8%), and provision of waterfowl and waterbird habitat (20.1%). Since it was not possible to identify the existence of Atlantic white cedar swamps, bald cypress swamps, and other uncommon wetland types, the function addressing the conservation of biodiversity could not be examined. Click on maps in Table 6 to see the extent and distribution of wetlands of potential significance for nine functions.

Table 6. Preliminary functional assessment results for Nanticoke wetlands at pre-settlement.

Function (Map)	Potential Significance	Pre-settlement Acreage	% of Total Wetland Acreage
Surface Water Detention (Map 5NW pre-settlement)	High Potential Moderate Potential	50,339.9 174,911.7	21.9 76.0
Streamflow Maintenance (Map 6NW pre-settlement)	High Potential Moderate Potential	180,238.8 1,349.5	78.4 0.6
Nutrient Transformation (Map 7NW pre-settlement)	High Potential Moderate Potential	96,353.9 133,665.3	41.9 58.1
Retention of Sediments and Inorganic Particulates (Map 8NW pre-settlement)	High Potential Moderate Potential	50,338.9 50,302.0	21.9 21.9
Coastal Storm Surge Detention (Map 9NW pre-settlement)	High Potential	33,561.6	14.6
Shoreline Stabilization (Map 10NW pre-settlement)	High Potential	50,507.4	22.0
Fish/Shellfish Habitat* (Map 11NW pre-settlement)	High Potential Shading Potential	26,354.9 16,765.4	11.5 7.3
Waterfowl/Waterbird Habitat (Map 12NW pre-settlement)	High Potential Wood Duck Potential	26,396.7 19,823.6	11.5 8.6
Other Wildlife Habitat (Map 13NW pre-settlement)	High Potential Moderate Potential	223,681.7 6,337.5	97.2 2.8

----

*Wetlands important for streamflow maintenance should also be recognized as vital to maintaining fish and shellfish habitat.

Contemporary Conditions (1998)

Wetlands were classified according to the U.S. Fish and Wildlife Service's official wetland classification system (Cowardin et al. 1979) and by landscape position, landform, and water flow path (LLWW) descriptors following Tiner (2003a). Wetland acreage summaries for the Nanticoke watershed are given in Tables 7 and 8 and wetland distribution is illustrated on 1998 Maps 1NW through 4NW. Table 7 summarizes wetland types through the subclass level of the Service's classification ("NWI types"), while Table 8 tabulates statistical data on wetlands by landscape position, landform , and water flow path ("LLWW types").

Wetlands by NWI Types

According to the NWI, in 1998 the Nanticoke watershed had 142,005 acres of wetlands, excluding linear features (Table 7; Map 1NW 1998). Eighty-eight percent of wetlands were palustrine wetlands. Palustrine forested wetlands accounted for nearly 85,000 acres or 68 percent of the palustrine wetlands. This figure excludes mixed forested/scrub-shrub and forested/emergent types and many of the other palustrine types (e.g., scrub-shrub/emergent wetlands) that represent forested wetlands in post-harvest succession. The overwhelming majority (93%) of palustrine wetlands was nontidal (beyond the influence of the tides); only 7 percent of the palustrine wetlands were subjected to periodic tidal flooding. Nearly 400 acres of other freshwater wetlands were tidally influenced; they were classified as riverine tidal wetlands (emergent and unconsolidated shore types). These wetlands represented only 0.2 percent of the Nanticoke's wetlands. Estuarine wetlands accounted for 12 percent of the watershed's wetlands. Irregularly flooded emergent wetlands predominated, occupying over 15,000 acres and representing about 91 percent of the Nanticoke's estuarine wetlands.

Note: The watershed also had 19,708 acres of deepwater habitats: 116,703 acres of estuarine waters, 1,832 acres of tidal rivers, 138 acres of nontidal rivers, and 1,035 acres of lacustrine waters (impounded lakes), excluding linear streams.

Table 7. Wetlands in the Nanticoke watershed in 1998 classified by NWI wetland type to the class level (Cowardin et al. 1979).

NWI Wetland Type	1998 Acreage
Estuarine Wetlands	
Emergent (Regularly Flooded)	640.2 (239.3 = oligohaline)
Emergent (Irregularly Flooded)	15,323.5 (6,100.2 = oligohaline)
Scrub-Shrub (Irregularly Flooded)	139.3 (85.3 = oligohaline)
Forested (Irregularly Flooded)	241.1
Unconsolidated Shore (Irregularly Exposed)	38.8
Unconsolidated Shore (Regularly Flooded)	535.2 (274.4 = oligohaline)
Total	*16,918.1 (6,699.2 = oligohaline)*
Palustrine Wetlands (nontidal, except where noted)	
Aquatic Bed	0.8
Emergent	1,457.9 (8.5 = Emergent/Forested)
Emergent (Tidal)	296.2
Mixed Emergent/Scrub-Shrub (Deciduous)	3,113.7
Mixed Emergent/Scrub-Shrub (Evergreen)	785.8
Farmed	3,527.8
Needle-leaved Deciduous Forested	79.9
Evergreen Forested	8,274.6 (67.1 = Atlantic White Cedar)
Evergreen Forested (Tidal)	107.9
Scrub-Shrub/Emergent	2,550.5
Broad-leaved Deciduous Forested	38,502.1 (187.8 = w/Bald Cypress)
Broad-leaved Deciduous Forested (Tidal)	7,169.8 (26.0 = w/Bald Cypress)
Mixed Forested	30,204.7
Mixed Forested (Tidal)	572.5
Deciduous Forested/Emergent	410.3 (23.4 = tidal)
Forested/Scrub-Shrub and Forested/Scrub-Shrub	13,992.5 (107.5 = tidal)
Deciduous Scrub-Shrub	2,115.6
Evergreen Scrub-Shrub	6,115.5
Mixed Scrub-Shrub	4,034.8
Scrub-Shrub (Tidal)	189.5
Unconsolidated Bottom/Vegetated	40.4 (34.8 = w/Bald Cypress)
Unconsolidated Bottom	1,157.0
Unconsolidated Shore	7.9
Total	*124,707.7*
Riverine Wetlands	
Emergent (Tidal)	332.0
Unconsolidated Shore (Tidal)	46.7
Total	*378.7*
GRAND TOTAL	142,004.5

Wetlands by LLWW Types[2]

Roughly 4,900 wetlands (excluding ponds) were inventoried in the Nanticoke River watershed and classified by their hydrogeomorphic features (Table 8). Terrene wetlands were the predominant type, comprising 78 percent of these wetlands (excluding ponds) and 72 percent of the watershed's wetland acreage (Map 2NW 1998). Lotic wetlands were second-ranked in number (17.5% of the wetlands) and were third-ranked in acreage (12.0% of the total acreage). Estuarine wetlands were second-ranked in acreage (16.1%) and third-ranked in number (2.9%). Lentic wetlands made up 1 percent of the wetland number and only 0.2 percent of the wetland acreage.

From the landform standpoint, interfluve wetlands accounted for 71 percent of the wetland acreage, followed by fringe wetlands (16.6%) and floodplain wetlands (10.6%) (Map 3NW 1998). Other wetland landforms accounted for less than two percent of the acreage (flats - 1.1%; basins - 0.5%, and islands - 0.2%).

Outflow wetlands were the predominant water flow path type, totaling 95,190 acres (67.6% of the wetland acreage; Map 4NW 1998). Bidirectional-tidal wetlands were second-ranked with 25,772 acres (18.3% of the total acreage), followed by throughflow wetlands with 10,532 acres (10.4%). Isolated wetlands accounted for 5,011 acres (3.6%) and bidirectional water flow wetlands associated with impoundments totaled only 260 acres (0.2%).

A total of 910 ponds were identified, occupying 1,289 acres. The average size of a pond was 1.4 acres. Over half of the pond acreage (51.1%) and nearly 40 percent of the number of ponds were represented by outflow ponds (658.8 acres for 335 ponds). Isolated ponds were most numerous (458 ponds, 443.1 acres), accounting for half of the ponds and slightly more than one-third of the pond acreage. The 117 throughflow ponds identified occupied almost 187 acres (14.5% of the pond acreage and 12.9% of the number of ponds). (Note: Pond acreage re: LLWW types is higher than based on NWI types because large sewage treatment lagoons were treated as ponds in the former and as lacustrine in the latter.)

The lakes present in the Nanticoke watershed were artificially created by damming rivers and streams or by excavation and diking activities. A total of 19 "lakes" covering nearly 904 acres were inventoried. The average size of a lake was 47.6 acres. Most (88.4%) of the lakes were throughflow lakes, while the rest were outflow lakes.

---

[2] All wetlands, except palustrine unconsolidated bottoms, were characterized by LLWW descriptors. These exceptions were classified as pond or lake types and are not reflected in the wetland summary statistics.

Table 8. Wetlands (excluding ponds) in the Nanticoke watershed in 1998 classified by landscape position, landform, and water flow path (Tiner 2003a). <u>Note</u>: Number of wetlands is approximate due to GIS processing.

Landscape Position	Landform	Water Flow	Approx. # of Wetlands	1998 Acreage (% of Grand Total)	
Estuarine	Fringe*	Bidirectional-tidal	143	22,384.5	(15.9)
	Island	Bidirectional-tidal	2	248.5	(0.2)
	Total		*145*	*22,633.0*	*(16.1)*
Lentic	Basin	Bidirectional	26	109.6	(0.1)
	Flat	Bidirectional	8	21.4	(<0.1)
	Fringe	Bidirectional	14	123.5	(0.1)
	Island	Bidirectional	4	5.0	(<0.1)
	Total		*52*	*259.5*	*(0.2)*
Lotic River	Floodplain	Bidirectional-tidal	151	2,364.3	(1.7)
		Throughflow	6	28.0	(<0.1)
	Fringe	Bidirectional-tidal	104	614.2	(0.4)
	Island	Bidirectional-tidal	1	0.3	(<0.1)
	Total		*262*	*3,006.8*	*(2.1)*
Lotic Stream					
	Basin	Throughflow	52	351.8	(0.2)
	Flat	Throughflow	95	779.6	(0.6)
	Floodplain	Throughflow	385	12,396.0	(8.8)
		Bidirectional-tidal	25	138.7	(0.1)
	Fringe	Throughflow	29	245.8	(0.2)
		Bidirectional-tidal	13	21.0	(<0.1)
	Total		*599*	*13,932.9*	*(9.9)*
Terrene	Basin	Isolated	7	14.8	(<0.1)
		Outflow	14	251.3	(0.2)
	Flat	Isolated	10	82.7	(0.1)
		Outflow	47	721.6	(0.5)
		Throughflow	1	1.0	(<0.1)
	Fringe	Outflow	1	1.0	(<0.1)
	Interfluve	Isolated	1551	4,913.4	(3.5)
		Outflow	2120	94,216.3	(66.9)
		Throughflow	111	813.2	(0.6)
	Total		*3,862*	*101,015.3*	*(71.7)*
GRAND TOTAL			4,920	140,847.5	

*Includes tidal freshwater wetlands contiguous with estuarine wetlands and along estuarine waters.

Most of the wetlands in the Nanticoke watershed performed four functions at significant levels (Table 9): surface water detention (96.9% of the wetland acreage), nutrient transformation (96.2%), provision of other wildlife habitat (96.2%), and streamflow maintenance (74.6%). About 30 percent of the wetland acreage was predicted to provide significant retention of sediments and other particulates and shoreline stabilization. One fourth of the acreage was estimated to be significant for the conservation of biodiversity in the watershed. Nearly three-quarters of this acreage was represented by two large predominantly forested areas that are probably important for forest-breeding birds of the Mid-Atlantic Region. About 23-24 percent of the total wetland acreage was predicted to provide important habitat for fish, shellfish, waterfowl and waterbirds. Click on maps in Table 9 to see the extent and distribution of wetlands of potential significance for each of the ten functions.

Table 9. Preliminary functional assessment results for Nanticoke wetlands in 1998. Ponds are included in this assessment.

Function (Map)	Potential Significance	1998 Acreage (total)	% of Total Wetland Acreage (total)
Surface Water Detention (Map 5NW 1998)	High Potential Moderate Potential	39,200.7 98,423.7 (137,624.4)	27.6 69.3 (96.9)
Streamflow Maintenance (Map 6NW 1998)	High Potential Moderate Potential	23,678.0 82,331.3 (106,009.3)	16.7 57.9 (74.6)
Nutrient Transformation (Map 7NW 1998)	High Potential Moderate Potential	35,756.1 100,934.9 (136,691.0)	25.2 71.0 (96.2)
Retention of Sediments and Other Particulates (Map 8NW 1998)	High Potential Moderate Potential	38,599.3 4,742.6 (43,341.9)	27.2 3.3 (30.5)
Coastal Storm Surge Detention (Map 9NW 1998)	High Potential	25,725.2	18.1
Shoreline Stabilization (Map 10NW 1998)	High Potential Moderate Potential	39,021.2 0.9 (39,022.1)	27.5 - (27.5)

Table 9. (cont'd)

Fish/Shellfish Habitat* (Map 11NW 1998)	High Potential	17,619.4	12.4
	Moderate Potential	1,413.5	1.0
	Shading Potential	13,161.8	9.3
		(32,194.7)	(22.7)
Waterfowl/Waterbird Habitat (Map 12NW 1998)	High Potential	18,122.4	12.8
	Moderate Potential	1,201.5	0.8
	Wood Duck Potential	14,739.6	10.4
		(34,063.5)	(24.0)
Other Wildlife Habitat (Map 13NW 1998)	High Potential	130,041.8	91.5
	Moderate Potential	6,666.8	4.7
		(136,708.6)	(96.2)
Biodiversity (Map 14NW 1998)	Atlantic White Cedar	119.6	0.1
	Bald Cypress	354.0	0.2
	Estuarine Oligohaline	6683.6	4.7
	Riverine Tidal	378.5	0.3
	Palustrine Tidal Emergent	373.5	0.3
	Palustrine Tidal Evergreen Forested	627.9	0.4
	Palustrine Tidal Scrub-Shrub	243.1	0.2
	Estuarine Forested	242.1	0.2
	Estuarine Scrub-Shrub	69.5	<0.1
	Palustrine Aquatic Bed**	0.8	<0.1
	Palustrine Emergent Seasonally Flooded	289.6	0.2
	Palustrine Semipermanently Flooded	317.1	0.2
	Palustrine Scrub-Shrub Seasonally Flooded	134.1	0.1
	Palustrine Evergreen Forested Seasonally Flooded	102.4	0.1
	Palustrine Forested/Emergent Seasonally Flooded	125.8	0.1
	Palustrine Forested/Broad-leaved Evergreen Seasonally Flooded	189.2	0.1
	Forested Complex #1	15,324.7	10.8
	Forested Complex #2	10,188.4	7.2
		(35,763.9)	(25.2)

*Wetlands important for streamflow maintenance are also vital for maintaining this habitat.
**Probably more extensive but not detected by this inventory due to source imagery.

Comparison: Pre-settlement Conditions vs. 1998 Conditions

Wetland Extent

The estimated acreage of wetlands in pre-settlement times was 230,019 acres (approximately 45% of the watershed). By 1998, wetland acreage declined to only 62 percent of the original acreage and many of these wetlands were altered (e.g., ditched, excavated, or impounded). In 1998, only 28 percent of the watershed was occupied by wetlands. Acreage of palustrine wetlands decreased by nearly 40 percent, while acreage of estuarine wetlands dropped by 28 percent due to sea level rise effects. Some of the loss of palustrine forested wetlands was also attributed to sea level rise and subsequent coastal subsidence that converted these forests to estuarine wetlands. This process is still occurring as witnessed by the presence of salt marsh vegetated growing with salt-stressed loblolly pines and the remains of woody plants in estuarine marshes. Most of the loss of palustrine wetlands, however, was due to conversion to agriculture, the predominant land use in the watershed today. Besides the outright elimination of wetlands, this conversion also caused fragmentation of the remaining wetlands. For example, at pre-settlement, there was an estimated 380 terrene interfluve outflow wetlands accounting for 72 percent of the wetlands; these wetlands had an average size of 433 acres. By 1998, this type had increased in number by nearly 6 times (to 2120) and decreased in acreage by 43 percent (to 94,216.3 acres), resulting in a reduction in the average size to 44 acres (just one tenth of its original average size).

Wetland Functions

Two comparisons of changes in functions were made, one showing changes in acres providing functions at significant levels (Table 10) and the other depicting changes in functional units (Table 11). From an acreage standpoint, substantial losses in wetlands providing all functions ranging from over 50 percent acreage loss in wetlands performing sediment retention to about 20 percent loss of wetlands stabilizing shorelines and providing coastal storm surge detention. Thirty percent of the wetland acreage performing most functions was lost. The streamflow maintenance function experienced the greatest change in performance. Ditching of terrene interfluve wetlands effectively drained many headwater wetlands converting them to cropland (upland) or significantly altered the hydrology of many remaining wetlands, thereby lowering their streamflow maintenance function from high to moderate. Eighty-seven percent of high-functioning streamflow maintenance acreage was lost, with 48 percent of this acreage converted to upland and 52 percent reduced to moderate potential.

When functional units were evaluated, the change in "functional capacity" can be better seen (Table 11). Roughly 64 percent of the functional capacity of wetlands contributing to streamflow maintenance was lost. This means that the watershed may be operating at only 36 percent of its pre-settlement capacity. The watershed's capacity for providing six other functions decreased by more than 25 percent (i.e., surface water detention, nutrient transformation, sediment and other particulate retention, fish and shellfish habitat, waterfowl and waterbird habitat, and other wildlife habitat). The two remaining functions (shoreline stabilization and coastal storm surge detention) were reduced by approximately 23 percent of their pre-settlement capacity. No function experienced an increase in capacity.

Table 10. Comparison of preliminary functional assessment results for Nanticoke wetlands at pre-settlement versus 1998. Acreage of function and percentage of the wetland total are given for each function.

Function	Potential Significance	Pre-settlement Acreage (% of total acreage)	1998 Acreage (% of total)	% Change in Acres
Surface Water Detention	High	50,339.9 (21.9)	39,200.7 (27.6)	-22.1
	Moderate	174,911.7 (76.0)	98,423.7 (69.3)	-43.7
Streamflow Maintenance	High	180,238.8 (78.4)	23,678.0 (16.7)	-86.9
	Moderate	1,349.5 (0.6)	82,331.3 (57.9)	+600.1%
Nutrient Transformation	High	96,353.9 (41.9)	35,756.1 (25.2)	-62.9
	Moderate	133,665.3 (58.1)	100,934.9 (71.0)	-24.5
Retention of Sediments and Other Particulates	High	50,338.9 (21.9)	38,599.3 (27.2)	-23.3
	Moderate	50,302.0 (21.9)	4,742.6 (3.3)	-90.6
Shoreline Stabilization	High	50,507.4 (22.0)	39,021.2 (27.5)	-22.7
	Moderate	-	0.9 (-)	+neglible
Coastal Storm Surge Detention	High	33,561.6 (14.6)	25,725.2 (18.1)	-23.3
Fish/Shellfish Habitat	High	26,354.9 (11.5)	17,619.4 (12.4)	-33.1
	Moderate	-	1,413.5 (1.0)	+signif
	Shading	16,765.4 (7.3)	13,161.8 (9.3)	-21.5
Waterfowl/Waterbird Habitat	High	26,396.7 (11.5)	18,122.4 (12.8)	-31.3
	Moderate	-	1,201.5 (0.8)	+signif
	Wood Duck	19,823.6 (8.6)	14,739.6 (10.4)	-25.6
Other Wildlife Habitat	High	223,681.7 (97.2)	130,041.8 (91.5)	-41.9
	Moderate	6,337.5 (2.8)	6,666.8 (4.7)	+5.2

Table 11. Predicted change in the Nanticoke watershed's capacity to perform nine wetland functions from pre-settlement to 1998. Functional units were derived from predictive values for each time period by applying a weighting scheme (2 for high; 1 for moderate; and 1 for other significant features, e.g., stream shading). The conservation of biodiversity function was not compared since original data lacked sufficient detail for such comparison.

Function	Pre-settlement Functional Units	1998 Functional Units	Predicted % Change in Functional Capacity
Surface Water Detention	275,591.5	176,825.1	-35.8
Streamflow Maintenance	361,827.1	129,687.3	-64.2
Nutrient Transformation	326,373.1	172,447.1	-47.2
Sediment and Other Particulate Retention	150,979.8	81,941.2	-45.7
Shoreline Stabilization	101,014.8	78,043.3	-22.7
Coastal Storm Surge Detention	67,123.2	51,450.4	-23.3
Fish and Shellfish Habitat	69,475.2	49,814.1	-28.3
Waterfowl and Waterbird Habitat	72,617.0	52,185.9	-28.1
Other Wildlife Habitat	453,700.9	266,750.4	-41.2

Natural Habitat Extent

At pre-settlement, the entire watershed (excluding river and stream bottoms) was in natural vegetation (Map 14NW pre-settlement). European settlement and the rise in human population led to the conversion of much of this natural habitat to land for human uses like farming, housing, and commercial/industrial facilities. By 1998, over half of the "natural" habitat (e.g., forests, thickets, vegetated wetlands, and non-agricultural fields) had been converted to agricultural land (235,000 acres or 46.5% of the watershed) and developed land (38,000 acres or 7.5%) (Map 15NW 1998).

Discussion

Extensive wetlands have always been recognized on the Delmarva Peninsula. Interpretation of the 1920s soil surveys predicted that the percent of the county represented by wetlands ranged from 32 percent for Caroline County to a high of 75 percent for Dorchester County (Table 12). The latter county had extensive tidal wetlands bordering Chesapeake Bay and much acreage of flatwood soils (e.g., Elkton). If the former are discounted, the extent of wetlands in the five-county area was between 40-50 percent. In the Nanticoke River watershed, an estimated 44 percent of the watershed was occupied by wetlands in the pre-settlement era. Today, only 28 percent of the watershed is wetland. Similarly, land use has converted much of the natural habitat of the watershed to agricultural land and to a lesser degree, developed (urban/suburban) land (see Map 15NW 1998). As of 1998 only 46 percent of the watershed was in "natural habitat" and that figure includes commercial forests as "natural habitat."

The pre-settlement estimate of estuarine wetlands is probably an overestimate since the rate of sea level rise appears to have only accelerated substantially over the past 100 years. Prior to this time, the rate of sea level rise was minimal or at least, low enough for marsh accretion to keep pace with the rising tides. The U.S.G.S. topographic maps displayed a 6-foot (2 m) depth contour as the shallowest depth line that could be used to approximate the lower limit of former estuarine wetlands (including tidal flats). Perhaps navigation charts may provide more detailed depth contours, but electronic versions were not available for the study area. Consulting historic maps might be beneficial but was not part of this study. Kearney et al. (1988) examined marsh loss in the Nanticoke River estuary and reported an average marsh loss of 0.5 percent (122.5 acres) annually since 1938, with higher rates in the lower estuary. Widening of tidal channels within the marshes also increased with channel width doubling in many creeks. Marsh loss appears to originate in the marsh interior with a merging of ponds and waterlogging of substrates. Today, only the upstream tidal marshes appear to be keeping pace with or exceeding the rate of sea level rise; downstream there seems to be little allochthonous sediment input, thereby creating an accretionary deficit relative to sea level. These marshes are in jeopardy and many acres may be converted to open water during the next 50-100 years.

For historic vegetation patterns, information comes from two sources: 1) The Plant Life of Maryland (Shreve et al. 1910) and 2) 1920s soil survey reports. Table 13 summarizes data from Shreve (1910), while Table 14 presents a list of plants associated with various soil types. For the latter, the list comes directly from the soil survey reports and one can usually determine what genus or species they are referring to; in a few cases, the common names are no longer used, so one would have to make a best guess, without doing more investigation. These reports also support our interpretation that essentially all of the soils were forested in their original state, except for tidal marsh.

More recent descriptions of wetland plant communities typical of the Nanticoke River watershed have been reported in NWI state reports for Delaware and Maryland (see Tiner 1985, Tiner and Burke 1995, respectively). Dominant trees of tidal swamps include red maple (*Acer rubrum*) and green ash (*Fraxinus pennsylvanica* var. *subintergerrima*). Black willow (*Salix nigra*) and black gum (*Nyssa sylvatica*) may co-dominate in places and large areas of tidal loblolly pine swamp (*Pinus taeda*) are common in Dorchester and Somerset Counties, Maryland (Tiner and Burke

1995). Seasonally flooded nontidal forested wetlands are usually represented by one or more of the following species: red maple, sweet gum (*Liquidambar styraciflua*), willow oak (*Quercus phellos*), pin oak (*Q. palustris*), basket or swamp chestnut oak (*Q. michauxii*), and loblolly pine. Temporarily flooded[3] or seasonally saturated wetland forests ("winter wet woods") are largely characterized by loblolly pine with various hardwoods including white oak (*Q. alba*), American beech (*Fagus grandifolia*), tulip or yellow poplar (*Liriodendron tulipifera*), American holly (*Ilex opaca*), red maple, and black gum. Red oak (*Q. rubra*) and southern red oak (*Q. falcata*) may also occur in significant numbers. Other seasonally saturated wetlands are wet deciduous forests dominated by red maple. black gum, and sweet gum. Associated trees include loblolly pine, American holly, sweet bay (*Magnolia virginiana*), willow oak, southern red oak, red oak, water oak (*Q. nigra*), and basket oak.

---

[3]Temporarily flooded wetlands noted in Tiner (1985) and Tiner and Burke (1995) are mostly represented by seasonally saturated types (a term not widely used until the mid-1990s - see footnote 2 page 91 in Tiner and Burke 1995).

Table 12. Acreage of wetlands in each county in the study area in the early 21st Century based on 1920s county soil surveys (Snyder et al. 1924, Dunn et al. 1920, Winant and Bacon 1929, Snyder and Gillett 1925, and Snyder et al. 1926). Note statistics are for the entire county not just the area within the Nanticoke River watershed.

County	Wetland Soils	Acreage	% of County	Source
Caroline	Elkton loam	21,632	10.6	
	Elkton sandy loam	7,424	3.6	
	Elkton silt loam	3,584	1.8	
	Plummer loamy sand	2,304	1.1	
	Portsmouth loam	7,872	3.9	
	Portsmouth sandy loam	7,424	3.6	
	Meadow	10,304	5.0	
	Tidal marsh	4,416	2.2	
	------------------------------	-----------	-----	
	Total	65,010	31.8	Winant and Bacon 1929
Dorchester	Elkton silt loam	161,536	43.8	
	Elkton sandy loam	12,800	3.5	
	Elkton loam	7,808	2.1	
	Meadow	5,056	1.4	
	Portsmouth loam	1.344	0.4	
	Tidal marsh	88,128	23.9	
	------------------------------	-----------	--------	
	Total	276,672	75.1	Snyder et al. 1926
Wicomico	Elkton sandy loam	19,648	8.1	
	Elkton silt loam	18,112	7.5	
	Elkton fine sandy loam	17,728	7.3	
	Elkton loam	10,944	4.5	
	Portsmouth f. sandy loam	18,432	7.6	
	Portsmouth loam	6,528	2.7	
	St. Johns sandy loam	6,272	2.6	
	Meadow	4,416	1.8	
	Swamp	6,784	2.8	
	Tidal marsh	15,168	6.3	
	------------------------------	--------------	------	
	Total	124,032	51.2	Snyder and Gillett 1925
Kent	Elkton sandy loam	51,392	13.5	
	Elkton loam	16,128	4.3	
	Elkton silt loam	12,096	3.2	
	Portsmouth sandy loam	17,920	4.7	
	Portsmouth silt loam	14,528	3.8	
	Portsmouth loam	6,400	1.7	
	Coastal beach	704	0.2	
	Meadow	8,512	2.2	
	Swamp	10,688	2.8	
	Tidal marsh	45,568	12.0	
	------------------------------	---------- -----		
	Total	183,936	48.4	Dunn et al. 1920

Table 12. (Continued)

County	Wetland Soils	Acreage	% of County	Source
Sussex	Elkton sandy loam	91,712	15.2	
	Elkton sand	7,488	1.2	
	Elkton loam	2,496	0.4	
	Portsmouth sandy loam	52,544	8.7	
	Portsmouth loam	17,344	3.0	
	St. Johns sand	960	0.1	
	Coastal beach	4,224	0.7	
	Meadow	3,392	0.6	
	Swamp	26,432	4.4	
	Tidal marsh	35,136	5.8	
	-------------------------	-----------	----	
	Total	241,728	40.1	Snyder et al. 1924

Table 13. Vegetation of Eastern Shore swamps and floodplains according to Shreve (1910). Major tree species are italicized. Common names generally follow Tiner (1988).

Wetland Type	Vegetation
Clay Upland Swamps	<u>Trees</u>: *sweet gum, white oak, black gum, willow oak, red maple, swamp white oak, loblolly pine*, American holly, and basket oak <u>Shrubs</u>: sweet pepperbush, maleberry, highbush blueberry, swamp azalea, fetterbush, southern arrowwood, Virginia sweet-spires, black haw, sweet bay, common winterberry, flowering dogwood, and smooth alder <u>Herbs</u>: sedges and pale manna grass <u>Others</u>: peat moss
Sandy Loam Upland Swamps	<u>Trees</u>: *loblolly pine, willow oak, white oak, sweet gum, red maple, water oak, basket oak, black gum, sweet bay, American holly, flowering dogwood*, fringe-tree, and river birch <u>Shrubs</u>: wax myrtle, southern arrowwood, poison sumac, staggerbush, Virginia sweet-spires, devil's walking stick, red chokeberry, and American strawberrybush <u>Herbs</u>: none specified <u>Others</u>: peat moss
Wetter Floodplain Forests	<u>Trees</u>: *red maple, black gum, white ash, and sweet bay* <u>Shrubs</u>: common winterberry, sweet pepperbush, smooth alder, southern arrowwood, buttonbush, and poison sumac <u>Herbs</u>: lizard's tail, cinnamon fern, sensitive fern, golden saxifrage, turtlehead, marsh St. John's-wort, jewelweed, sweet white violet, cursed crowfoot, bladder sedge, and sweet-scented bedstraw
Sandy Floodplains	<u>Trees</u>: *loblolly pine, water oak, American holly, black gum, sweet bay, white ash, fringe-tree, flowering dogwood, and ironwood* <u>Shrubs</u>: sweet pepperbush, southern arrowwood, pink azalea, and American strawberrybush <u>Herbs</u>: partridgeberry, bladder sedge, Long's sedge, and sedge <u>Vines</u>: common greenbrier, Virginia creeper, fox grape, trumpet creeper, and wild yam

Table 13. (cont'd)

Drier Floodplain
  Forests

Trees: *tulip poplar, ironwood, sweet gum, white ash, sycamore, American elm, willow oak, red maple, and black gum*
Shrubs: spicebush, southern arrowwood, and American strawberrybush
Herbs: Virginia grape fern, white grass, smooth Solomon's-seal, jack-in-the-pulpit, sweet white violet, swamp aster, and wood sorrel

Upland Swamps of the
  Wicomico Terrace

Trees: *black gum, swamp white oak, red maple, sweet gum, willow oak, white oak,* American holly, beech, sweet bay, and swamp cottonwood
Shrubs: Virginia sweet-spires, red chokeberry, and swamp azalea
Herbs: water smartweed, inflated bladderwort, and mermaid-weed

River Swamps

Trees: *bald cypress, black gum, red maple, sweet gum, swamp black gum, green ash, sweet bay,* tulip poplar, ironwood, swamp cottonwood, water oak, Atlantic white cedar, loblolly pine, white oak, and American holly
Shrubs: wax myrtle, sweet pepperbush, maleberry, smooth alder, buttonbush, silky dogwood, southern arrowwood, staggerbush, water-willow, and dangleberry
Vines: trumpet creeper, grapes, common greenbrier, Virginia creeper, poison ivy, and cross vine
Herbs: dwarf St. John's-wort, jewelweed, water pennywort, marsh St. John's-wort, marsh fern, cardinal flower, three-way sedge, water primrose, mermaid-weed, lizard's tail, false nettle, ditch stonecrop, Virginia bugleweed, and hoplike sedge

Stream Swamps

Trees (small-sized): *red maple, green ash,* loblolly pine, Atlantic white cedar, black gum, sweet bay, sweet gum, black willow, swamp white oak, and river birch
Shrubs: common winterberry, sweet pepperbush, buttonbush, smooth alder, water-willow, silky dogwood, Virginia sweet-spires, poison sumac, southern arrowwood, and swamp rose
Herbs: broad-leaved cattail, cinnamon fern, jewelweed, lizard's tail, royal fern, big-leaved arrowhead, water hemlock, water dock, arrow arum, pickerelweed, New York ironweed, water pepper, blue flag, mermaid-weed, tall meadow-rue, marsh blue violet, and false nettle

34

Table 14. Generalized plant-soil correlations from early 1900s soil survey reports.

County (Source)	Soil or Land Type	Characteristic Vegetation
Dorchester (Snyder et al. 1926)	Elkton sandy loam	Loblolly pine, oak, black gum, sweet gum, holly, myrtle, huckleberry, and bull brier (65-75% of this soil was forested with second growth)
	Elkton loam	Pine, oak, maple, gum, myrtle, and huckleberry (50% of this soil was forested with second growth)
	Elkton silt loam	Gum, soft maple, loblolly pine, oaks, holly, myrtle, huckleberry, with other "bushes and shrubs" (75% of this soil was forested with second growth)
	Elkton silt loam, low phase	Loblolly pine, maple, oak, holly, myrtle, huckleberry, grass, and "shrubs that thrive on a moist soil." (very little of this soil was cleared; averages 1.5-2-feet above sea level)
	Portsmouth loam	Pine, oak, black gum, sweet gum, huckleberry, bullberries, myrtle, and "other shrubs and grasses." (only a "very small part" was cultivated; rest is in forest)
	Meadow ("semiswampy alluvial soils")	Oak, pine, black gum, sweet gum, myrtle bushes, and briers (when in forest)
	Tidal marsh	Marsh grasses and a few shrubs or salt-water bushes
	Tidal marsh, low phase	Stunted pines, myrtle bushes, and marsh grasses
Wicomico (Snyder and Gillett 1925)	Elkton sandy loam	White oak, black oak, willow oak, water oak, black gum, sweet gum, pine, beech, maple, dogwood, myrtle, huckleberry, and other shrubs (a considerable amount of this soil was cultivated)
	Elkton fine sandy loam	Pine, white oak, sweet gum, black gum, huckleberry, myrtle, holly, smilax, and other shrubs and vines (some of this soil is cleared; most in forest)
	Elkton loam	White and black oaks, pine, beech, sweet gum, black gum, myrtle, huckleberry, smilax, and other vines and shrubs (probably 50% was in forest)
	Elkton silt loam	White, black, red, and willow oaks, sweet gum, black gum, loblolly pine, maple, beech, hickory ("white oak land"; a large part of this soil was forest)
	St. Johns sandy loam	Pine, oak, gum, holly, maple, myrtle, buckberry, smilax, and "other shrubs and vines that thrive on a moist soil" (65-75% was cultivated)
	Portsmouth fine sandy loam	Not listed (50% was forested; vegetation similar to "the other poorly drained soils")
	Portsmouth loam	Loblolly pine, hardwoods, myrtle, bay, huckleberry, smilax, and other vines and shrubs (most of this soil was forested)
	Meadow (poorly drained alluvial soil)	In its native state meadow supported a dense forest of "water-loving species"
	Swamp	No plants listed
	Tidal Marsh	Salt grasses and other "marsh-loving plants"
Caroline (Winant and Bacon 1929)	Elkton loam	Not listed (about 40-50% was cultivated)
	Elkton sandy loam	Not listed
	Elkton silt loam	Not listed (only a small portion was cultivated)
	Portsmouth loam	Not listed (no more than 35% was cultivated)

	Portsmouth sandy loam	Sweet gum, black gum, beech, maple, pine, huckleberry, gallberry, and other bushes (not more than 33% was cleared)
	Meadow	Alder, oak, pine, black gum, sweet gum, myrtle, and briers
	Tidal Marsh	Marsh grasses, numerous sedges, ironweed, cow lily, arrowhead, water hemp, and wild rice
Kent (Dunn et al. 1920)	Elkton sandy loam	Oaks (mostly white), black gum, sweet gum, maple, dogwood, and other trees (used extensively for agriculture but still much remained in timber)
	Elkton loam	White oak, willow oak, black gum, sweet gum, maple, and other deciduous trees ("white oak land"; over 50% forested)
	Elkton silt loam	White oak, willow oak, sweet gum, black gum, maple, hickory, red oak, and moss ("white oak land"; considerable portion was cultivated despite low agricultural value)
	Portsmouth sandy loam	Willow oak, swamp white oak, black gum, sweet gum, ash, maple, ironwood, chestnut, willow, azalea, buttonbush, high-bush huckleberry, and similar plants (large proportion of this soil was forest)
	Portsmouth loam	Willow oak, sweet gum, black gum, and alder (much of this soil was nonagricultural)
	Portsmouth silt loam	Vegetation like Portsmouth loam with denser underbrush (most remained in forest)
	Meadow	Water oak, spotted oak, maple, birch, alder, sweet gum, willow, ash, cat-brier, wild grape, and poison ivy (original state was forest)
	Swamp	Gum, willow, alder, cedar, pine, bay, birch, maple, and extremely dense undergrowth of brush, vines, and other plants adapted to swampy conditions
	Tidal Marsh	Cattails, swordgrass, calamus, and various "salt-loving and marsh-loving plants"
Sussex (Snyder et al. 1924)	Elkton sand	Pine, oak, maple, beech, and gum (about 50% was forest)
	Elkton sandy loam	White oak, black oak, willow oak, water oak, black gum, sweet gum, pine, beech, maple, dogwood, myrtle, huckleberry, and other shrubs (large part was farmed; rest was forest)
	Elkton loam	White oak, willow oak, black gum, sweet gum, maple and other deciduous trees ("white-oak land"; large part of this soil was forest)
	St. Johns sand	Pine, oak, gum, holly, maple, huckleberry, and other shrubs ("iron-mine land"; about 50% was forest)
	Portsmouth sandy loam	Loblolly pine, post oak, white oak, willow oak, water oak, sweet gum, holly, beech, maple, ash, bay, buttonbush, highbush huckleberry, myrtle, laurel, and smilax; cleared areas support dense growth of broom sedge (much of this soil was cleared and cultivated)
	Portsmouth loam	Pine, sweet gum, oak, maple, some cypress, briers, smilax, bay, huckleberry, and gallberry (only small areas cultivated)
	Meadow	Willow oak, white oak, black oak, sweet gum, alder, maple, birch, loblolly pine, smilax (catbrier or greenbrier), wild grape, and poison ivy
	Swamp	Pine, gum, birch, maple, alder, buttonbush, cedar, and dense growth of vines and shrubs (none of this was cultivated)
	Tidal Marsh	Swordgrass, calamus, cat-tails, and various "marsh-loving and salt-water plants"

Conclusions

Wetlands in the Nanticoke River watershed have undergone significant changes since pre-settlement. Prior to European colonization, about 45 percent of the watershed (roughly 230,000 acres) was wetland, with extensive headwater wetlands supporting streamflow. By 1998, only about 142,000 wetland acres (64% of the original acreage) remained and much of this acreage has been ditched, excavated, or impounded. Conversion of wetlands to agricultural lands was the predominant cause of wetland change since by 1998 about 46 percent of the watershed was in agricultural land use.

Cumulative wetland losses have led to significant reductions in many wetland functions. Since colonial times, it was estimated that the Nanticoke watershed lost over 60 percent of its predicted capacity for streamflow maintenance and over 30 percent of its capacity for four other functions: surface water detention, nutrient transformation, sediment and other particulate retention, and provision of other wildlife habitat. No function has experienced an increase in capacity.

The findings of this report provide an overview of the predicted changes in wetland extent and function for the Nanticoke River watershed since European settlement. The comparison of changes in wetland function watershed-wide should be considered approximate due to the nature of this type of analysis (e.g., reconstruction of pre-settlement wetland distribution from soils and topographic data). As with any remotely-sensed analysis, field checking should be conducted to validate the interpretations regarding functions of individual wetlands since this type of assessment is a coarse-filter approach and not a fine-filter one. Despite these limitations, the report serves as a foundation for understanding the extent to which wetlands have changed in general form and in function. As such, it provides a valuable tool for resource planning to be used with other tools (derived from field observations and other site-specific data) to help devise a watershed-wide strategy for wetland conservation and restoration.

Acknowledgments

This study was funded by the Kent Conservation District (KCD) and the Maryland Eastern Shore Resource Conservation and Development Council (ESRC&D). Project officers were Tim Riley for KCD and Dave Wilson for ESRC&D. Ralph Tiner was principal investigator for the Service and was responsible for study design, project oversight, analysis, and report preparation.

Herbert Bergquist (FWS) was responsible for digital database construction of historic wetlands, wetland classification, GIS analyses, and preparation of statistics and maps included in this report. Bobbi Jo McClain assisted in digital database construction during the early phase of this work. Correlations between wetland characteristics and wetland functions used to produce the preliminary assessment of wetland functions were prepared jointly by the Service, wetland specialists from Maryland and Delaware, and other wetland scientists.

Amy Jacobs (DNREC) and the Nanticoke wetland group she assembled reviewed the draft protocols for correlating wetland characteristics with wetland functions and provided recommendations to modify the selection criteria. Participants included David Bleil, Katheleen Freeman, Cathy Wazniak, Mitch Keiler, and Bill Jenkins (Maryland Department of Natural Resource); Julie LaBranche (Maryland Department of the Environment); Marcia Snyder, Dennis Whigham, and Don Weller (Smithsonian Environmental Research Center); Matt Perry and Jon Willow (U.S. Geological Survey); Mark Biddle (DNREC); and Peter Bowman (Delaware Natural Heritage Program). Amy Jacobs and David Bleil reviewed the draft report. Abby Rokosch (DNREC) provided copies of the texts of 1920s soil survey reports for Kent and Sussex Counties.

References

Brewer, J.E., G.P. Demas, and D. Holbrook. 1998. Soil Survey of Dorchester County, Maryland. U.S.D.A. Natural Resources Conservation Service, Washington, DC.

Brinson, M. M. 1993. A Hydrogeomorphic Classification for Wetlands. U.S. Army Corps of Engineers, Washington, DC. Wetlands Research Program, Technical Report WRP-DE-4.

Cowardin, L. M., V. Carter, F. C. Golet, and E. T. LaRoe. 1979. Classification of Wetlands and Deepwater Habitats of the United States. U.S. Fish and Wildlife Service, Washington, DC. FWS/OBS-79/31.

Dunn, J.E., J.M. Snyder, and E. Hoffecker. 1920. Soil Survey of Kent County, Delaware. U.S. Department of Agriculture. Government Printing Office, Washington, DC.

Hall, R.L. 1970. Soil Survey Wicomico County, Maryland. U.S.D.A. Soil Conservation Service, Washington, DC.

Ireland, W., Jr. and E.D. Matthews. 1974. Soil Survey of Sussex County, Delaware. U.S.D.A. Soil Conservation Service, Washington, DC.

Kearney, M.S., R.E. Grace, and J. C. Stevenson. 1988. Marsh loss in Nanticoke Estuary, Chesapeake Bay. The Geographical Review 78: 205-220.

Matthews, E.D. 1964. Soil Survey Caroline County, Maryland. U.S.D.A. Soil Conservation Service, Washington, DC.

Matthews, E.D., and W. Ireland, Jr. 1971. Soil Survey Kent County, Delaware. U.S.D.A. Soil Conservation Service, Washington, DC.

Meyer, J.L., L.A. Kaplan, D. Newbold, D.L. Strayer, C.J. Woltemade, J.B. Zedler, R. Beilfuss, Q. Carpenter, R. Semlitsch, M.C. Watzin, and P.H. Zedler. 2003. Where Rivers are Born: The Scientific Imperative for Defending Small Streams and Wetlands. American Rivers and Sierra Club, Washington, DC. 23 pp.

Mitsch, W.J. and J.G. Gosselink. 1993. Wetlands. Van Nostrand Reinhold, New York, NY.

Robbins, C.S., D.K. Dawson, and B.A. Dowell. 1989. Habitat area requirements of breeding forest birds of the Mid-Atlantic states. Wildlife Monogr. 103: 1-34.

Schroeder, R.L. 1996. Wildlife Community Habitat Evaluation Using a Modified Species-Area Relationship. U.S. Army Corps of Engineers, Waterways Expt. Station, Vicksburg, MS. Wetlands Research Program Tech. Rep. WRP-DE-12.

Shreve, F. 1910. The ecological plant geography of Maryland: Coastal Zone; Eastern Shore District. In: F. Shreve, M.A. Chrysler, F.H. Blodgett, and F.W. Besley. The Plant Life of Maryland. The John Hopkins Press, Baltimore, MD. pp. 101-148.

Snyder, J.M., J.H. Barton, J.E. Dunn, J. Gum, and W.A. Gum. 1924. Soil Survey of Sussex County, Delaware. U.S. Department of Agriculture, Bureau of Soils. Government Printing Office, Washington, DC.

Snyder, J.M. and R.L. Gillett. 1925. Soil Survey of Wicomico County, Maryland. U.S. Department of Agriculture, Bureau of Soils. Government Printing Office, Washington, DC.

Snyder, J.M., W.C. Jester, and O.C. Bruce. 1926. Soil Survey of Dorchester County, Maryland. U.S. Department of Agriculture, Bureau of Soils. Government Printing Office, Washington, DC.

Tiner, R.W. 1985. Wetlands of Delaware. U.S. Fish and Wildlife Service, National Wetlands Inventory Project, Newton Corner, MA and Delaware Department of Natural Resources and Environmental Control, Dover, DE. Cooperative publication.

Tiner, R.W. 1988. Field Guide to Nontidal Wetland Identification. Maryland Department of Natural Resources, Annapolis, MD and U.S. Fish and Wildlife Service, Northeast Region, Newton Corner, MA.

Tiner, R.W. 1997. NWI Maps: What They Tell Us. National Wetlands Newsletter 19(2): 7-12.

Tiner, R.W. 1998. In Search of Swampland: A Wetland Sourcebook and Field Guide. Rutgers University Press, New Brunswick, NJ.

Tiner, R.W. 1999. Wetland Indicators: A Guide to Wetland Identification, Delineation, Classification, and Mapping. Lewis Publishers, CRC Press, Boca Raton, FL.

Tiner, R. W. 2000. Keys to Waterbody Type and Hydrogeomorphic-type Wetland Descriptors for U.S. Waters and Wetlands (Operational Draft). U.S. Fish and Wildlife Service, Northeast Region, Hadley, MA.

Tiner, R.W. 2003a. Dichotomous Keys and Mapping Codes for Wetland Landscape Position, Landform, Water Flow Path, and Waterbody Type Descriptors. U.S. Fish and Wildlife Service, National Wetlands Inventory Program, Northeast Region, Hadley, MA.

Tiner, R.W. 2003b. Correlating Enhanced National Wetlands Inventory Data with Wetland Functions for Watershed Assessments: A Rationale for Northeastern U.S. Wetlands. U.S. Fish and Wildlife Servie, Northeast Region, Hadley, MA.

Tiner, R., M. Starr, H. Bergquist, and J. Swords. 2000. Watershed-based Wetland Characterization for Maryland's Nanticoke River and Coastal Bays Watersheds: A Preliminary Assessment. U.S. Fish and Wildlife Service, Northeast Region, Hadley, MA. NWI report.

Tiner, R.W., H.C. Bergquist, J.Q. Swords, and B.J. McClain. 2001. Watershed-based Wetland Characterization for Delaware's Nanticoke River Watershed: A Preliminary Assessment Report. U.S. Fish and Wildlife Service, National Wetlands Inventory Program, Northeast Region, Hadley, MA. NWI report.

Tiner, R.W. and D.G. Burke. 1995. Wetlands of Maryland. U.S. Fish and Wildlife Service, Ecological Services, Northeast Region, Hadley, MA and Maryland Department of Natural Resources, Annapolis, MD. Cooperative National Wetlands Inventory publication.

Winant, H.B. and S.R. Bacon. 1929. Soil Survey of Caroline County, Maryland. U.S. Department of Agriculture, Bureau of Chemistry and Soils. Government Printing Office, Washington, DC.

Appendices

Appendix A.

Dichotomous Keys and Mapping Codes for Wetland Landscape Position, Landform, Water Flow Path, and Waterbody Type Descriptors (Tiner 2003a).

U.S. Fish and Wildlife Service

Dichotomous Keys and Mapping Codes for Wetland Landscape Position, Landform, Water Flow Path, and Waterbody Type Descriptors

September 2003

Dichotomous Keys and Mapping Codes for Wetland Landscape Position, Landform, Water Flow Path, and Waterbody Type Descriptors

Ralph W. Tiner
Regional Wetland Coordinator

U.S. Fish and Wildlife Service
National Wetlands Inventory Project
Northeast Region
300 Westgate Center Drive
Hadley, MA 01035

September 2003

This report should be cited as:

Tiner, R.W. 2003. Dichotomous Keys and Mapping Codes for Wetland Landscape Position, Landform, Water Flow Path, and Waterbody Type Descriptors. U.S. Fish and Wildlife Service, National Wetlands Inventory Program, Northeast Region, Hadley, MA. 44 pp. (original version; this attachment = 43 pp.)

Table of Contents

Page

Section 1. Introduction

A wide variety of wetlands have formed across the United States. To describe this diversity and to inventory wetland resources, government agencies and scientists have devised various wetland classification systems (Tiner 1999). Features used to classify wetlands include vegetation, hydrology, water chemistry, origin of water, soil types, landscape position, landform (geomorphology), wetland origin, wetland size, and ecosystem form/energy sources.

The U.S. Fish and Wildlife Service's wetland and deepwater habitat classification (Cowardin et al. 1979) is the national standard for wetland classification. This classification system emphasizes vegetation, substrate, hydrology, water chemistry, and certain impacts (e.g., partly drained, excavated, impounded, and farmed). These properties are important for describing wetlands and separating them into groups for inventory and mapping purposes and for natural resource management. They do not, however, include some abiotic properties important for evaluating wetland functions (Brinson 1993). Moreover, the classification of deepwater habitats is limited mainly to general aquatic ecosystem (marine, estuarine, lacustrine, and riverine) and bottom substrate type, with a few subsystems noted for riverine deepwater habitats. The Service's classification system would benefit from the application of additional descriptors that more fully encompass the range of characteristics associated with wetlands and deepwater habitats.

In the early 1990s, Mark Brinson created a hydrogeomorphic (HGM) classification system to serve as a foundation for wetland evaluation (Brinson 1993). He described the HGM system as "a generic approach to classification and not a specific one to be used in practice" (Brinson 1993, p. 2). This system emphasized the location of a wetland in a watershed (its geomorphic setting), its sources of water, and its hydrodynamics. The system was designed for evaluating similar wetlands in a given geographic area and for developing a set of quantifiable characteristics for "reference wetlands" rather than for inventorying wetland resources (Smith et al. 1995). A series of geographically focused models or "function profiles" for various wetland types have been created and are in development for use in functional assessment (e.g., Brinson et al. 1995, Ainslie et al. 1999, Smith and Klimas 2002).

Need for New Descriptors

The Service's National Wetlands Inventory (NWI) Program has produced wetland maps for 91 percent of the coterminous United States and 35 percent of Alaska. Digital data are available for 46 percent of the former area and for 18 percent of the latter. Although these data represent a wealth of information about U.S. wetlands, they lack hydrogeomorphic and other characteristics needed to perform assessments of wetland functions over broad geographic areas. Using geographic information system (GIS) technology and geospatial databases, it is now possible to predict wetland functions for watersheds - a major natural resource planning unit. Watershed managers could make better use of NWI data if additional descriptors (e.g., hydrogeomorphic-type attributes) were added to the current NWI database. Watershed-based preliminary assessments of wetland functions could be performed. This new information would also permit

1

more detailed characterizations of wetlands for reports and for developing scientific studies and lists of potential reference wetland sites.

Background on Development of Keys

Since the Cowardin et al. wetland classification system (1979) is the national standard and forms the basis of the most extensive wetland database for the country, it would be desirable to develop additional modifiers to enhance the current data. This would greatly increase the value of NWI digital data for natural resource planning, management, and conservation. Unfortunately, Brinson's "A Hydrogeomorphic Classification of Wetlands" (1993) was not designed for use with the Service's wetland classification. He used some terms from the Cowardin et al. system but defined them differently (e.g., Lacustrine and Riverine). Consequently, the Service needed to develop a set of hydrogeomorphic-type descriptors that would be more compatible with its system. Such descriptors would bridge the gap between these two systems, so that NWI data could be used to produce preliminary assessments of wetland functions based on characteristics identified in the NWI digital database. In addition, more descriptive information on deepwater habitats would also be beneficial. For example, identification of the extent of dammed rivers and streams in the United States is a valuable statistic, yet according to the Service's classification dammed rivers are classified as Lacustrine deepwater habitats with no provision for separating dammed rivers from dammed lacustrine waters. Differentiation of estuaries by various properties would also be useful for national or regional inventories.

Recognizing the need to better describe wetlands from the abiotic standpoint in the spirit of the HGM approach, the Service developed a set of dichotomous keys for use with NWI data (Tiner 1997b). The keys bridge the gap between the Service's wetland classification and the HGM system by providing descriptors for landscape position, landform, water flow path and waterbody type (LLWW descriptors) important for producing better characterizations of wetlands and deepwater habitats. The LLWW descriptors for wetlands can be easily correlated with the HGM types to make use of HGM profiles when they become available. The LLWW attributes were designed chiefly as descriptors for the Service's existing classification system (Cowardin et al. 1979) and to be applied to NWI digital data, but they can be used independently to describe a wetland or deepwater habitat.

The first set of dichotomous keys was created to improve descriptions of wetlands in the northeastern United States (Tiner 1995a, b). They were initially used to enhance NWI data for predicting functions of potential wetland restoration sites in Massachusetts (Tiner 1995a, 1997a). Later, the keys were modified for use in predicting wetland functions for watersheds nationwide (Tiner 1997b, 2000). A set of keys for waterbodies was added to improve the Service's ability to characterize wetland and aquatic resources for watersheds.

The keys are periodically updated based on application in various physiographic regions. This version is an update of an earlier set of keys published in 1997 and 2000 (Tiner 1997b, 2000). Relatively minor changes have been made, including the following: 1) added "drowned river-mouth" modifier to the Fringe and Basin landforms (for use in areas where rivers empty into large lakes such as the Great Lakes where lake influences are significant), 2) added "connecting

2

channels" to river type (to address concerns in the Great Lakes to highlight such areas), 3) added "Throughflow-intermittent" water flow path (to separate throughflow wetlands along intermittent streams from those along perennial streams), 4) added "Throughflow-artificial" and "Outflow-artificial" to water flow path (to identify former "isolated" wetlands or fragmented wetlands that are now throughflow or outflow due to ditch construction), 5) revised the lake key to focus on permanently flooded deepwater sites (note: shallow and seasonally to intermittently flooded sites are wetlands) and added "open embayment" modifier, and 6) revised the estuary type key (consolidated some types). This version also clarifies that a terrene wetland may be associated with a stream where the stream does not periodically flood the wetland. In this case, the stream has relatively little effect on the wetland's hydrology. This is especially true for numerous flatwood wetlands. It also briefly discusses how the term "isolated" is applied relative to surface water and ground water interactions. In the near future, illustrations will be added to this document to aid users in interpretations.

Use of the Keys

Two sets of dichotomous keys (composed of pairs of contrasting statements) are provided - one for wetlands and one for waterbodies. Vegetated wetlands (e.g., marshes, swamps, bogs, flatwoods, and wet meadows) and periodically exposed nonvegetated wetlands (e.g., mudflats, beaches, and other exposed shorelines) should be classified using the wetland keys, while the waterbody keys should be used for permanent deep open water habitats (subtidal or >6.6 feet deep for nontidal waters). Some sites may qualify as both wetlands and waterbodies. A good example is a pond. Shallow ponds less than 20 acres in size meet the Service's definition of wetland, but they are also waterbodies. Such areas can be classified as both wetland and waterbody, if desirable. However, we recommend that ponds be classified using the waterbody keys. Another example would be permanently flooded aquatic beds in the shallow water zone of a lake. We have classified them using wetland hydrogeomorphic descriptors, yet they also clearly represent a section of the lake (waterbody). This approach has worked well for us in producing watershed-based wetland characterizations and preliminary assessments of wetland functions.

Uses of Enhanced Digital Database

Once they are added to existing NWI digital data, the LLWW characteristics (e.g., landscape position, landform, water flow path, and waterbody type) may be used to produce a more complete description of wetland and deepwater habitat characteristics for watersheds. The enhanced NWI digital data may then be used to predict the likely functions of individual wetlands or to estimate the capacity of an entire suite of wetlands to perform certain functions in a watershed. Such work has been done for several watersheds including Maine's Casco Bay watershed and the Nanticoke River and Coastal Bays watersheds in Maryland, the Delaware portion of the Nanticoke River, and numerous small watersheds in New York (see Tiner et al. 1999, 2000, 2001; Machung and Forgione 2002; Tiner 2002; see sample reports on the NWI website:http://wetlands.fws.gov for application of the LLWW descriptors). These characterizations are based on our current knowledge of wetland functions for specific types (Tiner 2003) and may be refined in the future, as needed, based on the applicable HGM profiles and other information. The new terms can also be used to describe wetlands for reports of various kinds including wetland permit reviews, wetland trend reports, and other reports requiring more comprehensive descriptions of individual wetlands.

Organization of this Report

The report is organized into seven sections: 1) Introduction, 2) Wetland Keys, 3) Waterbody Keys, 4) Coding System for LLWW Descriptors (codes used for classifying and mapping wetlands), 5) Acknowledgments, 6) References, and 7) Glossary.

Section 2. Wetland Keys

Three keys are provided to identify wetland landscape position and landform for individual wetlands: Key A for classifying the former and Keys B and C for the latter (for inland wetlands and coastal wetlands, respectively). A fourth key - Key D - addresses the flow of water associated with wetlands. Table 1 lists the LLWW descriptors. It gives readers a good idea of what the various combinations may be. Also see wetland codes in one of the following sections.

Users should first identify the landscape position associated with the subject wetland following Key A-1. Afterwards, using Key B-1 for inland wetlands and Key C-1 for salt and brackish wetlands, users will determine the associated landform. The landform keys include provisions for identifying specific regional wetland types such as Carolina bays, pocosins, flatwoods, cypress domes, prairie potholes, playas, woodland vernal pools, West Coast vernal pools, interdunal swales, and salt flats. Key D-1 addresses water flow path descriptors. Various other modifiers may also be applied to better describe wetlands, such as headwater areas; these are included in the four main keys.

Besides the keys provided, there are numerous other attributes that can be used to describe the condition of wetlands. Some examples are other descriptors that address resource condition could be ones that emphasize human modification, (e.g., natural vs. altered, with further subdivisions of the latter descriptor possible), the condition of wetland buffers, or levels of pollution (e.g., no pollution [pristine], low pollution, moderate pollution, and high pollution). Addressing wetland condition, however, was beyond our immediate goal of describing wetlands from a hydrogeomorphic standpoint.

Table 1. List of landscape position, landform, water flow path, and waterbody type (LLWW) descriptors. Note that more detailed categorization of landforms and pond types are possible through the use of modifiers, but they have not been shown here.

Landscape Position	Landform	Water Flow Path	Waterbody Type
Marine	Fringe Island	Bidirectional-tidal	Open Ocean Reef-protected Waters Atoll Lagoon Fjord Semi-protected Oceanic Bay
Estuarine	Fringe Basin Basin (tidally restricted) Island	Bidirectional-tidal	Fjord Island Protected Rocky Headland Bay Rocky Headland Bay Tectonic Estuary River-dominated Estuary Drowned River Valley Estuary Bar-built Estuary Bar-built Estuary (Coastal Pond) Bar-built Esturay (Hypersaline Lagoon) Island-protected Estuary Shoreline Bay Estuary

Lotic	Floodplain
	Basin
	Flat
	Fringe
	Island
		Throughflow
		Throughflow-intermittent
		Throughflow-entrenched
		Bidirectional-tidal
			River (Gradients: Tidal, Dammed, High,
			  Middle, Low, and Intermittent)
			Stream (Gradients: Tidal, Dammed, High,
			  Middle, Low, and Intermittent)

6

Lentic	Fringe	Bidirectional-nontidal	Natural Lake (Main body, Open Embayment, Semi-enclosed Embayment, Barrier Beach Lagoon)
	Basin	Bidirectional-tidal	Dammed River Valley Lake (Reservoir)
	Flat	Throughflow	Dammed River Valley Lake (Hydropower)
	Island		Dammed River Valley Lake (Other)
			Other Dammed Lake (Former Natural Lake)
			Other Dammed Lake (Artificial Lake)
			Pond (numerous types)
Terrene	Fringe (pond)	Outflow	
	Basin	Outflow-artificial	
	Basin (former floodplain)	Inflow	
	Flat	Throughflow	
	Flat (former floodplain)	Throughflow-artificial	
	Interfluve	Throughflow-entrenched	
	Slope	Isolated	
		Paludified	

7

Key A-1: Key to Wetland Landscape Position

This key characterizes wetlands based on their location in or along a waterbody, in a drainageway, or in isolation.

1. Wetland is located in or along tidal salt or brackish waters (i.e., an estuary or ocean) including its periodically inundated shoreline (excluding areas formerly under tidal influence)...................2
1. Wetland is not located in or along these waters...3

2. Wetland is located along shores of the cean..**Marine**
                                                       Go to Key C-1 for coastal landform
2. Wetland is located in or along an estuary (e.g., typically a semi-enclosed basin or tidal river where fresh water mixes with sea water)..**Estuarine**
                        Go to Key E-2 for Estuary Type, then to Key C-1 for coastal landform

> Note: If area was formerly connected to estuary but now is completely cut-off from tidal flow, consider as one of inland landscape positions - Terrene, Lentic, or Lotic, depending on current site characteristics. Such areas should be designated with a modifier to identify such wetlands as "former estuarine wetland." Lands overflowed infrequently by tides such as overwash areas on barrier islands are considered an Estuarine. Tidal freshwater wetlands contiguous to salt/brackish/oligohaline tidal marshes are also considered Estuarine, whereas similar wetlands just upstream along strictly fresh tidal waters are considered Lotic.

3. Wetland is located in or along a lake or reservoir (permanent waterbody where standing water is typically much deeper than 6.6 feet at low water), including streamside wetlands in the lake basin and wetlands behind barrier islands and beaches with open access to the lake............**Lentic**
                                                       Go to Key C-2 for Lake Type
                                                Then *Go to Key B-1 for inland landform*

> Note: Lentic wetlands consist of all wetlands in a lake basin, including those bordering streams that empty into the lake. The upstream limit of lentic wetlands is defined by the upstream influence of the lake which is usually approximated by the limits of the basin within which the lake occurs. The streamside lentic wetlands are designated as "Throughflow," thereby emphasizing the stream flow through these wetlands. Other lentic wetlands are typically classified as "Bidirectional Flow" since water tables rise and fall with lake levels during the year. Tidally-influenced freshwater lakes have "Bidirectional Tidal" flow.
>
> *Modifiers*: Natural, Dammed River Valley, Other Dammed - see Key C-2 for others.

3. Wetland does not occur along this type of waterbody...4

4. Wetland is located in or along a river or stream (flowing water), including in-stream ponds and wetlands on the active floodplain and it is subjected to periodic flooding.....................................5

8

4. Wetland occurs on a slope or flat, or in a depression (including ponds, potholes, and playas) lacking a stream <u>or</u> is situated on a historic (inactive) floodplain; may be connected to other wetlands or waters through ditches; also includes flatwoods with streams but streams do not periodically inundate the wetland..**Terrene**

Go to Key B-1 for inland landform

Modifiers may include <u>Headwater</u> (for first-order streams, possibly second-order streams also; including large wetlands in upper portion of watershed believed to be significant groundwater discharge sites important to streamflow) and for terrene wetlands whose outflow goes directly to an estuary or the ocean: <u>Estuarine Outflow</u> or <u>Marine Outflow</u>, respectively.

5. Wetland is the source of a river or stream but this waterbody does not extend through the wetland..**Terrene**
5. Wetland is in or along a river or stream, or on its active floodplain...6

6. Wetland is in or along a river (a broad channel mapped as a polygon or 2-lined watercourse on a 1:24,000 U.S. Geological Survey topographic map), or on its active floodplain........**Lotic River**
6. Wetland is in or along a stream (a.linear or single line watercourse on a 1:24,000 U.S. Geological Survey topographic map), or on its active floodplain..............................**Lotic Stream**

Go to Couplet "a" below

(Also see note under first couplet #3 - Lentic re: streamside wetlands in lake basins)

<u>Note</u>: Artificial drainageways--ditches--are not considered part of the Lotic classification, whereas channelized streams are part of the Lotic landscape position.

Modifiers: <u>Headwater</u> (first order streams, possibly second order streams and large wetlands in upper portion of watershed believed to be significant groundwater discharge sites) and <u>Channelized</u> (excavated and/or stream course modified).

a. Water flow is under tidal influence (freshwater tidal areas)....................**Tidal Gradient**

Go to Key B-1 for inland landform

a. Water flow is not under tidal influence (nontidal)...b

b. Water flow is dammed, yet still flowing downstream, at least seasonally.....................
....**Dammed Reach**

Go to Key B-1 for inland landform

Modifiers: Lock and Dammed, Run-of-River Dam, Beaver Dam, and Other Dam (see Waterbody Key B-2 for further information).

b. Water flow is unrestricted..c

c. Water flow is intermittent during the year...................................**Intermittent Gradient**

Go to Key B-1 for inland landform

9

c. Water flow is perennial (year-round)..d

d. Water flow is generally rapid due to steep gradient; typically little or no floodplain development; watercourse is generally shallow with rock, cobbles, or gravel bottoms; first and second order "streams"; part of Cowardin's Upper Perennial and Intermittent subsystems..**High Gradient**

Go to Key B-1 for inland landform

d. Watercourse characteristics are not so; "stream" order greater than 2...........................e

e. Water flow is generally slow; typically with extensive floodplain; water course shallow or deep with mud or sand bottoms; typically fifth and higher order "streams", but includes lower order streams in nearly level landscapes such as the Great Lakes Plain (former glacial lakebed) and the Coastal Plain (the latter streams may lack significant floodplain development) and ditches; Cowardin's Lower Perennial subsystem............**Low Gradient**

Go to Key B-1 for inland landform

e. Water flow is fast to moderate; with little to some floodplain; usually third and fourth order "streams"; part of Cowardin's Upper Perennial subsystem.............**Middle Gradient**

Go to Key B-1 for inland landform

Key B-1: Key to Inland Landforms

1. Wetland occurs on a noticeable slope (e.g., greater than a 2 percent slope)........**Slope Wetland**
Go to Key D-1 for water flow path

Modifiers can be applied to Slope Wetlands to designate the type of inflow or outflow as <u>Channelized Inflow or Outflow</u> (intermittent or perennial, stream or river), <u>Nonchannelized Inflow or Outflow</u> (wetland lacking stream, but connected by observable surface seepage flow), or <u>Nonchannelized-Subsurface Inflow or Outflow</u> (suspected subsurface flow from or to a neighboring wetland upslope or downslope, respectively).

1. Wetland does not occur on a distinct slope...2

2. Wetland forms an island...**Island Wetland**
(Go to Key D-1 for water flow path)

<u>Note</u>: Can designate an island formed in a delta at the mouth of a river or stream as a <u>Delta Island Wetland</u>; other islands are associated with landscape positions (e.g., lotic river island wetland, lotic stream island wetland, lentic island wetland, or terrene island pond wetland). Vegetation class and subclass from Cowardin et al. 1979 should be applied to characterize the vegetation of these wetland islands; vegetation is assumed to be rooted unless designated by a *modifier* – "<u>Floating Mat</u>" to indicate a floating island.

2. Wetland does not form an island...3

3. Wetland occurs within the banks of a river or stream or along the shores of a pond, lake, or island, or behind a barrier beach or island, <u>and</u> is <u>either</u>: (1) vegetated *and* typically permanently inundated, semipermanently flooded (including their tidal freshwater equivalents plus seasonally flooded-tidal palustrine emergent wetlands which tend to be flooded frequently by the tides) or otherwise flooded for most of the growing season, or permanently saturated due to this location <u>or</u> (2) a nonvegetated bank or shore that is temporarily or seasonally flooded .....**Fringe Wetland**
Go to Couplet "a" below for Types of Fringe Wetlands
Then *Go to Key D-1 for water flow path*
<u>Attention</u>: *Seasonally to temporarily flooded vegetated wetlands along rivers and streams (including tidal freshwater reaches) are classified as either Floodplain, Basin, or Flat landforms - see applicable categories.*

    a. Wetland forms along the shores of an upland island within a lake, pond, river, or stream...b
    a. Wetland does not form along the shores of an island.......................................d

    b. Wetland forms behind a barrier island or beach spit along a lake..............<u>Lentic Barrier Island Fringe Wetland</u> or <u>Lentic Barrier Beach Fringe Wetland</u>
        Modifier: <u>Drowned River-mouth</u>
    b. Wetland forms along another type of island...c

c. Wetland forms along an upland island in a river or stream.................<u>Lotic River Island</u> <u>Fringe Wetland</u> or <u>Lotic Stream Island Fringe Wetland</u>
c. Wetland forms along an upland island in a lake or pond.................<u>Lentic Island Fringe</u> <u>Wetland</u> or <u>Terrene Pond Island Fringe Wetland</u>

d. Wetland forms in or along a river or stream.........................<u>Lotic River Fringe Wetland</u> or <u>Lotic Stream Fringe Wetland</u>
d. Wetland forms in or along a pond or lake..e

e. Wetland forms along a pond shore...f
e. Wetland forms along a lake shore...<u>Lentic Fringe Wetland</u>
    Modifier: <u>Drowned River-mouth</u>

f. Wetland occurs along an in-stream pond.......................................<u>Lotic River or Stream</u> <u>Fringe Pond Wetland Throughflow</u>
f. Wetland occurs in another type of pond.............................<u>Terrene Fringe Pond Wetland</u>

<u>Note</u>: Vegetation is assumed to be rooted unless designated by a *modifier* to indicate a floating mat (<u>Floating Mat</u>).

3. Wetland does not exist along these shores...4

4. Wetland occurs on an active floodplain (alluvial processes in effect)........................**Floodplain** **Wetland*** (could specify the river system, if desirable).   *<u>Go to Key D-1 for water flow path</u>* Sub-landforms are listed below.

a. Wetland forms along the shores of a river island....................<u>Floodplain Island Wetland</u>
a. Wetland is not along an island...b

b. Wetland forms in a depressional feature on a floodplain........<u>Floodplain Basin Wetland</u> or <u>Floodplain Oxbow Wetland</u> (a special type of depression)
b. Wetland forms on a broad nearly level terrace..........................<u>Floodplain Flat Wetland</u>

*<u>Note</u>: Questionable floodplain areas may be verified by consulting soil surveys and locating the presence of alluvial soils, e.g., Fluvaquents or Fluvents, or soils with Fluvaquentic subgroups. While most Floodplain wetlands will have a Throughflow water flow path; others may be designated, e.g., Inflow, Outflow, or Isolated. Former floodplain wetlands are classified as Basins or Flats and designated as former floodplain.

Modifiers: <u>Partly Drained</u>; <u>Confluence wetland</u> - wetland at the intersection of two or more streams; <u>River-mouth</u> or <u>stream-mouth wetland</u> - wetland at point where a river and stream empties into lake; <u>Meander scar wetland</u> - floodplain basin wetland, the remnant of a former river meander.

4. Wetland does not occur on an active floodplain..5

5. Wetland occurs on an interstream divide (interfluve)...................................**Interfluve Wetland** or specify *regional types* of interfluve wetlands, for example: *Carolina Bay Interfluve Wetland, Pocosin Interfluve Wetland,* and *Flatwood Interfluve Wetland* (Southeast). Sub-landforms are listed below.   *Go to Key D-1 for water flow path*

> a. Wetland forms in a depressional feature................................. Interfluve Basin Wetland
> a. Wetland forms on a broad nearly level terrace ....Interfluve Flat Wetland

> *Modifiers*: Partly Drained.

5. Wetland does not occur on an interfluve..6

6. Wetland exists in a distinct depression in various positions on the landscape (i.e., surrounded by upland, along smaller rivers and streams, along in-stream ponds, along lake shores, or on former floodplains or interfluves)............ **Basin Wetland** or **Basin Wetland Former Floodplain** (including *Basin Oxbow Wetland Former Floodplain*) or **Basin Wetland Former Interfluve**. Can specify regional types: *Carolina Bay Basin Wetland* and *Pocosin Basin Wetland* (Atlantic Coastal Plain), *Cypress Dome Basin Wetland* (Florida), *Prairie Pothole Basin Wetland* (Upper Midwest), *"Salt Flat" Basin Wetland* (arid West), *Playa Basin Wetland* (Southwest), *West Coast Vernal Pool Basin Wetland* (California and Pacific Northwest), *Interdunal Basin Wetland* (sand dunes), *Woodland Vernal Pool Basin Wetland* (forests throughout the country), *Polygonal Basin Wetland* (Alaska), *Sinkhole Basin Wetland* (karst/limestone regions), *Pond Wetland Basin* (throughout country), or some type of *Island Basin Wetland* for basin wetlands on islands.
                                                                  Go to Key D-1 for water flow path

> *Modifiers* may be applied to indicate artificially created basins due to beaver activity or human actions or artificially drained basins including: Beaver (beaver-created); wetlands created for various purposes or unintentionally formed due to human activities - may want to specify purpose like Aquaculture (e.g., fish and crayfish), Wildlife management (e.g., waterfowl impoundments), and Former floodplain, or to designate former salt marsh that is now nontidal (Former estuarine wetland). Other *modifiers* may be applied to designate the type of inflow or outflow as Channelized (intermittent or perennial, stream or river), Nonchannelized-wetland (contiguous wetland lacking stream), or Nonchannelized-subsurface flow (suspected subsurface flow to neighboring wetland), or to identify a headwater basin (Headwater) or a drainage divide wetland that discharges into two or more watershed (Drainage divide), or to denote a spring-fed wetland (Spring-fed), a wetland bordering a pond (Pond basin wetland) and a wetland bordering an upland island in a pond (Pond island border). For lotic basin wetlands, consider additional modifiers such as Confluence wetland - wetland at the intersection of two or more streams; River-mouth or Stream-mouth wetland - wetland at point where a river and a stream empties into a lake. For lentic basins associated with the Great Lakes, possibly identify Drowned River-mouth wetlands where mouth extends into the lake basin. Partly drained may be used for ditched/drained wetlands.

6. Wetland exists in a relatively level area...**Flat Wetland**
or specify *regional types* of flat wetlands, for example: **Salt Flat Wetland** (in the Great Basin)
or flats that are fragments of once-larger interfluve flats or former floodplains: **Flat Wetland,
Former Interfluve** or **Flat Wetland, Former Floodplain**.

Go to Key D-1 for water flow path

Note: If desirable, a *modifier* for drained flats can be applied (Partly drained). Other
modifiers can be applied to designate the type of inflow or outflow as Channelized
(intermittent or perennial, stream or river), Nonchannelized-wetland (contiguous wetland
lacking stream), or Nonchannelized-subsurface flow (suspected subsurface flow to
neighboring wetland). For lotic flat wetlands, consider additional modifiers such as
confluence wetland - wetland at the intersection of two or more streams; river-mouth or
stream-mouth wetland - wetland at point where a river and a stream empties into a lake.

Key C-1: Key to Coastal Landforms

1. Wetland forms a distinct island in an inlet, river, or embayment.......................**Island Wetland**

Go to Key D-1 for water flow path

a. Occurs in a delta...Delta Island Wetland
(Could identify flood delta and ebb delta islands for tidal inlets if desirable.)
a. Occurs elsewhere either in a river or an embayment ....b

b. Occurs in a river..River Island Wetland
b. Occurs in a coastal embayment...Bay Island Wetland

1. Wetland does not form such an island, but occurs behind barrier islands and beaches, or along
the shores embayments, rivers, streams, and islands...2

2. Wetland occurs along the shore, contiguous with the estuarine waterbody.......**Fringe Wetland**

Go to Key D-1 for water flow path

a. Occurs behind a barrier island or barrier beach spit..........Barrier Island Fringe Wetland
or Barrier Beach Fringe Wetland [*Modifier* for overwash areas: Overwash]
a. Occurs elsewhere...b

b. Occurs along a coastal embayment or along an island in a bay........Bay Fringe Wetland
or Bay Island Fringe Wetland or Coastal Pond Fringe Wetland (a special type of
embayment, typically with periodic connection to the ocean unless artificially connected
by a bulkheaded inlet) or Coastal Pond Island Fringe Wetland
b. Occurs elsewhere..c

c. Occurs along a coastal river or along an island in a river...............River Fringe Wetland
or River Island Fringe Wetland

c. Occurs elsewhere...d

d. Occurs along an oceanic island...Ocean Island Fringe Wetland
d. Occurs along the shores of exposed rocky mainland...............Headland Fringe Wetland

2. Wetland is separated from main body of marsh by natural or artificial means; the former may be connected by a tidal stream extending through the upland or by washover channels (e.g., estuarine intertidal swales), whereas the latter occurs in an artificial impoundment or behind a road or railroad embankment where tidal flow is at least somewhat restricted........**Basin Wetland**
Go to Key D-1 for water flow path

Modifiers may be applied to separate natural from created basins (managed <u>fish and wildlife</u> areas; <u>aquaculture</u> impoundments; <u>salt hay</u> diked lands; <u>tidally restricted-road</u>, and <u>tidally restricted-railroad</u>), and for other situations, as needed.

Key D-1: Key to Water Flow Paths

1. Wetland is periodically flooded by tides...**Bidirectional-tidal**
    See Key F-2 for additional descriptors based on tidal ranges.
1. Wetland is not flooded by tides..2

2. Wetland is subject to fluctuating water levels due to lake influences....**Bidirectional-nontidal**

    <u>Note</u>: Lentic wetlands with streams running through them are best classified as Throughflow to emphasize this additional water source, while lentic wetlands located in coves or fringing the high ground would typically be classified as Bidirectional-Nontidal.

2. Wetland is not subject to lake influences..3

3. Wetland is formed by paludification processes where in areas of low evapotranspiration and high rainfall, peat moss moves uphill creating wetlands on hillslopes (i.e., wetland develops upslope of primary water source)..**Paludified**
3. Wetland is not formed by paludification processes...4

4. Wetland receives surface or ground water from a stream, other waterbody or wetland (i.e., at a higher elevation) <u>and</u> surface or ground water passes through the subject wetland to a stream, another wetland, or other waterbody at a lower elevation; a flow-through system...**Throughflow, Throughflow-intermittent*, Throughflow-entrenched*, or Throughflow-artificial***

    Modifiers: <u>Groundwater-dominated</u> throughflow wetlands can be separated from <u>Surface water-dominated</u> throughflow wetlands.

    *<u>Note</u>: **Throughflow-intermittent** is to be used with throughflow wetlands along intermittent streams; **Throughflow-entrenched** indicates that stream flow is through a

15

wetland but the stream is deeply cut and does not overflow into the wetland (therefore the stream is, for practical purposes, separate from the wetland) - this water flow path is intended to be used with Terrene wetlands in this situation; **Throughflow-artificial** is used to designate wetlands where throughflow is human-caused - usually to indicate connection of Terrene wetlands to other Terrene wetlands and waters by ditches and not by streams either natural or channelized

4. Water does not pass through this wetland to other wetlands or waters....................................5

5. There is no surface or groundwater inflow from a stream, other waterbody, or wetland (i.e., no documented surface or ground water inflow from a wetland or other waterbody at a higher elevation) <u>and</u> no observable or known outflow of surface or ground water to other wetlands or waters..**Isolated**

<u>Attention</u>: *In most applications, isolation is interpreted as "geographically isolated" since groundwater connections are typically unknown for specific wetlands. For practical purposes then," isolated" means no obvious surface water connection to other wetlands and waters. If hydrologic data exist for a locale that documents groundwater linkages, such wetlands should be identified as either outflow. inflow, or throughflow with a "<u>Groundwater-dominated</u>" modifier and not be identified as isolated <u>unless</u> the whole network of wetlands is not connected to a stream or river. In the latter case, the network is a collection of interconnected isolated wetlands.*

5. Wetland is not hydrologically or geographically isolated...6

6. Wetland receives surface or ground water inflow from a wetland or other waterbody (perennial or intermittent) at a higher elevation <u>and</u> there is no observable or known significant outflow of surface or ground water to a stream, wetland or waterbody at a lower elevation ....**Inflow**

> *Modifiers*: <u>Groundwater-dominated</u> inflow wetlands can be separated from <u>Surface water-dominated</u> inflow wetlands; <u>Human-caused</u> (usually to indicate connection of Terrene wetlands to other Terrene wetlands and waters [e.g., Inflow human-caused] by ditches and not by streams either natural or channelized).

6. Wetland receives no surface or ground water inflow from a wetland or permanent waterbody at a higher elevation (may receive flow from intermittent streams only) <u>and</u> surface or ground water is discharged from this wetland to a stream, wetland, or other waterbody at a lower elevation...**Outflow** or **Outflow-artificial***

> *Modifiers:* <u>Groundwater-dominated</u> outflow wetlands can be separated from <u>Surface water-dominated</u> outflow wetlands.

> *<u>Note</u>: Outflow-artificial is usually used to indicate outflow from formerly isolated wetlands resulting by ditches.

Section 3. Waterbody Keys

These keys are designed to expand the classification of waterbodies beyond the system and subsystem levels in the Service's wetland classification system (Cowardin et al. 1979). Users are advised first to classify the waterbody in one of the five ecosystems: 1) marine (open ocean and associated coastline), 2) estuarine (mixing zone of fresh and ocean-derived salt water), 3) lacustrine (lakes, reservoirs, large impoundments, and dammed rivers), 4) riverine (undammed rivers and tributaries), and 5) palustrine (e.g., nontidal ponds) and then apply the waterbody type descriptors below.

Five sets of keys are given. Key A-2 helps describe the major waterbody type. Key B-2 identifies different stream gradients for rivers and streams. It is similar to the subsystems of Cowardin's Riverine system, but includes provisions for dammed rivers to be identified as well as a middle gradient reach similar to that of Brinson's hydrogeomorphic classification system. The third key, Key C-2, addresses lake types, while Keys D-2 and E-2 further define ocean and estuary types, respectively. Key F-2 is a key to water flow paths of waterbodies. Key G-2 is for describing general circulation patterns in estuaries. The coastal terminology applies concepts of coastal hydrogeomorphology.

Besides the keys provided, there are numerous other attributes that can be used to describe the condition of waterbodies. Some examples are other descriptors that address resource condition could be ones that emphasize human modification, (e.g., natural vs. altered, with further subdivisions of the latter descriptor possible), the condition of waterbody buffers (e.g., stream corridors), or levels of pollution (e.g., no pollution [pristine], low pollution, moderate pollution, and high pollution).

Key A-2. Key to Major Waterbody Type

1. Waterbody is predominantly flowing water..2
1. Waterbody is predominantly standing water..7

> Note: Fresh waterbodies may be tidal; if so, waterbody is classified as a <u>Tidal Lake</u> or <u>Tidal Pond</u> using criteria below to separate lakes from ponds.

2. Flow is unidirectional and waterbody is a river, stream, or similar channel............................3
2. Flow is tidal (bidirectional) at least seasonally; waterbody is an ocean, embayment, river, stream, or lake..4

3. Waterbody is a polygonal feature on a U.S. Geological Survey map or a National Wetlands Inventory Map (1:24,000/1:25,000)..**River**
3. Waterbody is a linear feature on such maps..**Stream**
> *Go to River/Stream Gradient Key - Key B-2 - for other modifiers*

4. Waterbody is freshwater..5
4. Waterbody is salt or brackish...6

5. Waterbody is a polygonal feature on a U.S. Geological Survey map or a National Wetlands Inventory Map (1:24,000/1:25,000)..**River**
5. Waterbody is a linear feature on such maps..**Stream**
> *Go to River/Stream Gradient Key - Key B-2 - for other modifiers*

6. Part of a major ocean or its associated embayment (Marine system of Cowardin et al. 1979) ....**Ocean**

> *Go to Ocean Key - Key D-2*

6. Part of an estuary where fresh water mixes with salt water (Estuarine system of Cowardin et al. 1979)..**Estuary**

> *Go to Estuary Key - Key E-2*

7. Waterbody is freshwater..8
7. Waterbody is salt or brackish and tidal...10

8. Waterbody is permanently flooded and deep (>than 6.6 ft at low water), excluding small "kettle or bog ponds" (i.e., usually less than 5 acres in size and surrounded by bog vegetation)..**Lake**

> *Go to Lake Key - Key C-2*

8. Waterbody is shallow (< 6.6 ft at low water) or a small "kettle or bog pond" (with deeper water)..9

9. Waterbody is small (< 20 acres)..**Pond**

> Separate <u>natural</u> from <u>artificial</u> ponds, then add other modifiers like the following. Some *examples* of modifiers for ponds: <u>beaver, alligator, marsh, swamp, vernal, Prairie Pothole, Sandhill, sinkhole/karst, Grady, interdunal, farm-cropland, farm-livestock, golf, industrial, sewage/wastewater treatment, stormwater, aquaculture-catfish, aquaculture-shrimp, aquaculture-crayfish, cranberry, irrigation, aesthetic-business, acid-mine, arctic polygonal, kettle, bog, woodland, borrow pit, Carolina bay, tundra, coastal plain, tidal,</u> and <u>in-stream</u>.

> <u>Note</u>: Wetlands associated with ponds are typically either Terrene basin wetlands, such as a Cypress dome or cypress-gum pond, or Terrene pond fringe wetlands, such as semipermanently flooded wetlands along margins of pond. In-stream ponds are in the Lotic landscape position.

9. Waterbody is large (≥20 acres)..**Lake**

Go to Lake Key - Key C-2

10. Part of a major ocean or its associated embayment (Marine system of Cowardin et al. 1979) ....**Ocean**

Go to Ocean Key - Key D-2

10. Part of an estuary where fresh water mixes with salt water (Estuarine system of Cowardin et al. 1979)..**Estuary**

Go to Estuary Key - Key E-2

Key B-2. River/Stream Gradient and Other Modifiers Key

Please note that the river/stream gradient extends from the freshwater tidal zone through the intermittent reach. The limits of the latter are typically defined by drainageways with well-defined channels that discharge water seasonally. From a practical standpoint, the limits of the lotic system are displayed on 1:24,000 U.S. Geological Survey topographic maps or similar digital data. Intermittent streams, certain dammed portions of rivers plus lock and dammed canal systems may be classified as rivers using the descriptors presented in these keys. In the Cowardin et al. system, they may be classified as Riverine Intermittent Streambed or Lacustrine Unconsolidated Bottom, respectively.

1. Water flow is under tidal influence..**Tidal Gradient**

Type of tidal river or stream: 1) <u>natural river</u>, 2) <u>natural stream</u>, 3) <u>channelized river</u>, 4) <u>channelized stream</u>, 5) <u>canal</u> (artificial polygonal lotic feature), 6) <u>ditch</u> (artificial linear lotic feature), 7) <u>restored river segment</u> (part of river where restoration was performed), and 8) <u>restored stream segment</u> (part of stream where restoration was performed).

1. Water flow is not under tidal influence (nontidal)..2

2. Water flow is dammed, yet still flowing downstream at least seasonally..........**Dammed Reach**

       Type of dammed river: 1) <u>lock and dammed</u> (canalized river, a series of locks and dams are present to aid navigation), 2) <u>run-of-river dammed</u> (low dam allowing flow during high water periods; often used for low-head hydropower generation), and 3) <u>other dammed</u> (unspecified, but not major western hydropower dam as such waterbodies are considered lakes, e.g., Lake Mead and Lake Powell).

2. Water flow is unrestricted...3

3. Water flow is perennial (year-round); perennial rivers and streams...........................4
3. Water flow is seasonal or aperiodic (intermittent); Cowardin's Intermittent Subsystem........
....**Intermittent Gradient***

4. Water flow is generally rapid due to steep gradient; typically little or no floodplain development; watercourse is generally shallow with rock, cobbles, or gravel bottoms; first and second order "streams"; part of Cowardin's Upper Perennial subsystem...............**High Gradient***
4. Water flow is not so; some to much floodplain development.....................................5

5. Water flow is generally slow; typically with extensive floodplain; water course shallow or deep with mud or sand bottoms; typically fifth and higher order "streams", but includes lower order streams in nearly level landscapes such as the Great Lakes Plain (former glacial lakebed) and the Coastal Plain (the latter streams may lack significant floodplain development); Cowardin's Lower Perennial subsystem ....**Low Gradient***
5. Water flow is fast to moderate; with little to some floodplain; usually third and fourth order "streams"; part of Cowardin's Upper Perennial subsystem...............................**Middle Gradient***

**Type of river or stream* - additional modifiers that may be applied as desired: 1) <u>natural river-single thread</u> (one channel), 2) <u>natural river-multiple thread (braided)</u> (multiple, wide, shallow channels), 3) <u>natural river-multiple thread (anastomosed)</u> (multiple, deep narrow channels), 4) <u>natural stream-single thread</u>, 5) <u>channelized river</u> (dredged/excavated), 6) <u>channelized stream</u>, 7) <u>canal</u> (artificial polygonal lotic feature), 8) <u>ditch</u> (artificial linear lotic feature), 9) <u>restored river segment</u> (part of river where restoration was performed), 10) <u>restored stream segment</u> (part of stream where restoration was performed), and 11) <u>connecting channel</u> (joins two lakes). Other possible descriptors: 1) for perennial rivers and streams - <u>riffles</u> (shallow, rippling water areas), <u>pools</u> (deeper, quiet water areas), and <u>waterfalls</u> (cascades), 2) for water depth of perennial rivers - <u>deep rivers</u> ($\geq$6.6 ft at low water) from <u>shallow rivers</u> (<6.6 ft at low water), 3) nontidal river or stream segment emptying into an estuary, ocean, or lake (<u>estuary-discharge</u>, <u>ocean-discharge</u>, or <u>lake-discharge</u>), 4) classification by stream order (1st, 2nd, 3rd, etc. for perennial segments), and 5) channels patterns (straight, slight meandering, moderate meandering, and high meandering).

Key C-2. Key to Lakes.

The lake designation is for permanently flooded deep waters (>6.6 feet). Some classification systems include shallow waterbodies or periodically exposed areas as "lakes." The Cowardin et al. system considers standing waterbodies larger than 20 acres to be part of the lacustrine system (regardless of water depth; shallow = wetlands; >6.6 feet = deepwater habitat), and smaller ones typically part of the palustrine wetlands. For our purposes, "shallow lakes" and "seasonal or intermittent lakes" are considered some type of terrene or lotic wetland depending on the presence and location of a stream. Lentic wetlands are associated with permanently flooded standing waterbodies deeper than 6.6 feet at low water.

1. Waterbody is not dammed or impounded...**Natural Lake**

> *Modifiers*: Main body, Open embayment, Semi-enclosed embayment, Barrier beach lagoon, Seiche-influenced, River-fed and Stream-fed descriptors. Can also use applicable modifiers listed under Pond (see Key A-2).
>
> *Can use additional modifiers listed under Pond (see Key A-2) and others (e.g., crater, lava flow, aeolian, fjord, oxbow, other floodplain, glacial, alkali, and manmade), as appropriate.

1. Waterbody is dammed, impounded, or excavated 2

2. Waterbody is dammed or impounded...3
2. Waterbody is excavated...**Excavated Lake**
3. Dammed river valley...**Dammed River Valley Lake**

> *Modifiers*: Reservoir, Hydropower, and Seiche-influenced; also River-fed and Stream-fed descriptors.
>
> Note: When the dam inundates former floodplains and other low-lying areas, the waterbody is considered a Dammed River Valley Lake. If the dam crosses a higher gradient river and increase water depth in an channel without significant flooding of much neighboring "land," the waterbody is considered the dammed reach of a river.

3. Dammed natural lake or other landscape..**Other Dammed Lake**

> *Modifiers*: Former natural lake, Artificial lake, River-fed and Stream-fed descriptors.

Key D-2. Ocean Key.

1. Waterbody is completely open, not protected by any feature.................................**Open Ocean**
       (Can further identify <u>open bays</u> if desirable.)
1. Waterbody is somewhat protected...2

2. Associated with coral reef or island 3

2. Not associated with coral reef or island..4

3. Open but protected by coral reef .... **Reef-protected Waters**
3. Protected by a coral island.. **Atoll Lagoon**

4. Deep embayment cut by glaciers, with an underwater sill at front end, restricting circulation;
associated with rocky headlands...**Fjord**
4. Other semi-protected embayment..**Semi-protected Oceanic Bay**

      Modifiers for all types above: <u>Submerged vegetation</u> (e.g., eelgrass or turtle-grass) or
      <u>Floating vegetation</u> (e.g., macroalgae such as kelp beds).

Key E-2. Estuary Key.

The following types should encompass most of the estuaries located in the United States. There
may be estuaries that do not fit within this classification. Such types should be brought to the
attention of the author.

1. Estuary is surrounded by rocky headlands and shores...2
1. Estuary is not surrounded by rocky headlands and shores...4
2. Deep embayment cut by glaciers, with an underwater sill at front end, restricting circulation
(e.g., Puget Sound)..**Fjord Estuary**
2. Not so, either open or semi-enclosed...3

3. Protected by islands...................................**Island Protected Rocky Headland Bay Estuary**
3. Not protected by islands...**Rocky Headland Bay Estuary**

      Modifiers: <u>Open</u> or <u>Semi-enclosed</u>

4. Estuary is tectonically formed (e.g., San Franciso Bay), including volcanic activity................
....**Tectonic Estuary**

      Modifiers: <u>Fault-formed</u> and <u>Volcanic-formed</u>

4. Estuary is not tectonically formed or is formed by volcanic activity..5

5. Estuary is river-dominated with very little tidal range and a delta formed at the mouth of the river where it enters the sea (e.g., Mississippi River Delta)....................**River-dominated Estuary**
5. Estuary is not river-dominated...6

6. Estuary is a drowned river valley (e.g., Chesapeake Bay)........**Drowned River Valley Estuary**

   Modifiers: Open Bay, River Channel, and Semi-enclosed Bay

6. Estuary is not a drowned river valley...7

7. Estuary formed behind and is protected by sandy barrier islands or barrier beaches
(spits)...**Bar-built Estuary**

   Modifiers: Coastal Pond (oligohaline to saline) and Hypersaline Lagoon (hypersaline)

7. Estuary is not behind sandy barrier islands or beaches..8

8. Estuary is protected by reefs or other islands......................................**Island Protected Estuary**
8. Estuary is an open or semi-enclosed embayment....................................**Shoreline Bay Estuary**

Modifiers for all estuarine waterbodies: Inlet (includes any ebb- or flood- deltas that are completed submerged), Stabilized Inlet, Shoal (shallow water area), Submerged vegetation (e.g., eelgrass or turtle-grass) or Floating vegetation (e.g., macroalgae such as kelp beds).

Key F-2. Key to Water Flow Paths

1. Water flow is tidally influenced..2
1. Water flow is not under the influence of the tides..4

2. Tide range is greater than 4m (approx. >12 feet) ....**Macrotidal**
2. Tidal range is less than 4m 3

3. Tidal range is 2-4m (approx. 6-12 feet) ....**Mesotidal**
3. Tidal range is less than 2m (approx. < 6 feet) ....**Microtidal**

4. Water flows out of the waterbody via a river, stream, or ditch, with little or no inflow (inflow could be from intermittent streams or ground water only) ....**Outflow**

   Modifier: Human-caused for inflow via a ditch network.

4. Water flow is not so...5

5. Water enters waterbody from river, stream, or ditch, flows through it, and continues to flow downstream..**Throughflow** or **Throughflow-intermittent**

   Modifier: Human-caused for throughflow via a ditch network

   Note: Throughflow intermittent is applied to intermittent streams

5. Water flow is not throughflow...6

6. Water flow enters via a river, stream, or ditch, but does not exit pond, lake or reservoir; waterbody serves as a sink for water...**Inflow**

   Modifier: Human-caused for inflow via a ditch network.

6. No apparent channelized inflow, source of water either by precipitation or by underground sources..**Isolated**

Attention: *In most applications, isolation is interpreted as "geographically isolated" since groundwater connections are typically unknown for specific waterbodies. For practical purposes then," isolated" means no obvious surface water connection to other wetlands and waters. If hydrologic data exist for a locale that document groundwater linkages, such waterbodies should be identified as either outflow. inflow, or throughflow with a "Groundwater-dominated" modifier added and not be identified as isolated unless the whole network of waterbodies is not connected to a stream or river. In the latter case, the network is a collection of interconnected isolated waterbodies.*

Key G-2. Key to Estuarine Hydrologic Circulation Types

1. Estuary is river-dominated with distinct salt wedge moving seasonally up and down the river; fresh water at surface with most saline waters at bottom; low energy system with silt and clay bottoms ....**Salt-wedge Estuary**
1. Estuary is not river-dominated 2

2. Estuarine water is well-mixed, no significant salinity stratification, salinity more or less the same from top to bottom of water column; high-energy system with sand bottom.............. ....**Homogeneous Estuary**
2. Estuarine water is partially mixed, salinities different from top to bottom, but not strongly stratified; low energy system ....**Partially Mixed Estuary**

Section 4. Coding System for LLWW Descriptors

The following is the coding scheme for expanding classification of wetlands and waterbodies beyond typical NWI classifications. When enhancing NWI maps/digits, codes should be applied to all mapped wetlands and deepwater habitats (including linears). At a minimum, landscape position (including lotic gradient), landform, and water flow path should be applied to wetlands, and waterbody type and water flow path to water to waterbodies. Wetland and deepwater habitat data for specific estuaries, lakes, and river systems could be added to existing digital data through use of geographic information system (GIS) technology.

Codes for Wetlands

Wetlands are typically classified by landscape position, landform, and water flow path. Landforms are grouped according to Inland types and Coastal types with the latter referring to tidal wetlands associated with marine and estuarine waters. Use of other descriptors tends to be optional. They would be used for more detailed investigations and characterizations.

Landscape Position

ES	Estuarine
LE	Lentic
LR	Lotic river
LS	Lotic stream
MA	Marine
TE	Terrene

Lotic Gradient

1	Low
2	Middle
3	High
4	Intermittent
5	Tidal
6	Dammed
a	lock and dammed
b	run-of-river dam
c	beaver
d	other dammed
7	Artificial (ditch)

Lentic Type

1		Natural deep lake (see also Pond codes for possible specific types)
a		main body
b		open embbayment
c		semi-enclosed embayment
d		barrier beach lagoon
2		Dammed river valley lake
a		reservoir
b		hydropower
c		other
3		Other dammed lake
a		former natural
b		artificial
4		Excavated lake
a		quarry lake
5		Other artificial lake

Estuary Type

1		Drowned river valley estuary
a		open bay (fully exposed)
b		semi-enclosed bay
c		river channel
2		Bar-built estuary
a		coastal pond-open
b		coastal pond-seasonally closed
c		coastal pond-intermittently open
d		hypersaline lagoon
3		River-dominated estuary
4		Rocky headland bay estuary
a		island protected
5		Island protected estuary
6		Shoreline bay estuary
a		open (fully exposed)
b		semi-enclosed
7		Tectonic
a		fault-formed
b		volcanic-formed
8		Fjord
9		Other

Inland Landform

SL   Slope
 SLpa   Slope, paludified

IL   Island*
 ILde   Island, delta
 ILrs   Island, reservoir
 ILpd   Island, pond

FR   Fringe*
 FRil   Fringe, island*
 FRbl   Fringe, barrier island
 FRbb   Fringe, barrier beach
 FRpd   Fringe, pond
 FRdm   Fringe, drowned river mouth

FP   Floodplain
 FPba   Floodplain, basin
 FPox   Floodplain, oxbow
 FPfl   Floodplain, flat
 FPil   Floodplain, island

IF   Interfluve
 IFba   Interfluve, basin
 IFfl   Interfluve, flat

BA   Basin
 BAcb   Basin, Carolina bay
 BApo   Basin, pocosin
 BAcd   Basin, cypress dome
 BApp   Basin, prairie pothole
 BApl   Basin, playa
 BAwc   Basin, West Coast vernal pool
 BAid   Basin, interdunal
 BAwv   Basin, woodland vernal
 BApg   Basin, polygonal
 BAsh   Basin, sinkhole
 BApd   Basin, pond
 BAgp   Basin, grady pond
 BAsa   Basin, salt flat
 BAaq   Basin, aquaculture (created)
 BAcr   Basin, cranberry bog (created)
 BAwm   Basin, wildlife management (created)
 BAip   Basin, impoundment (created)

BAfe	Basin, former estuarine wetland
BAff	Basin, former floodplain
BAfi	Basin, former interfluve
BAfo	Basin, former floodplain oxbow
BAdm	Basin, drowned river-mouth

FL   Flat

FLsa	Flat, salt flat
FLff	Flat, former floodplain
FLfi	Flat, former interfluve

*Note: Inland slope wetlands and island wetlands associated with rivers, streams, and lakes are designated as such by the landscape position classification (e.g., lotic river, lotic stream, or lentic), therefore no additional terms are needed here to convey this association.

Coastal Landform

IL   Island

ILdt	Island, delta
ILde	Island, ebb-delta
ILdf	Island, flood-delta
ILrv	Island, river
ILst	Island, stream
ILby	Island, bay

DE   Delta

DEr	Delta, river-dominated
DEt	Delta, tide-dominated
DEw	Delta, wave-dominated

FR   Fringe

FRal	Fringe, atoll lagoon
FRbl	Fringe, barrier island
FRbb	Fringe, barrier beach
FRby	Fringe, bay
FRbi	Fringe, bay island
FRcp	Fringe, coastal pond
FRci	Fringe, coastal pond island
FRhl	Fringe, headland
FRoi	Fringe, oceanic island
FRlg	Fringe, lagoon
FRrv	Fringe, river island
FRst	Fringe, stream
FRsi	Fringe, stream island

BA   Basin
 BAaq   Basin, aquaculture (created)
 BAid   Basin, interdunal (swale)
 BAst   Basin, stream
 BAsh   Basin, salt hay production (created)
 BAtd   Basin, tidally restricted/road (not a management area)
 BAtr   Basin, tidally restricted/railroad (not a management area)
 BAwm   Basin, wildlife management (created)
 BAip   Basin, impoundment (created)

Water Flow Path

 PA   Paludified
 IS   Isolated
 IN   Inflow
 OU   Outflow
 OA   Outflow-artificial*
 TH   Throughflow
 TA   Throughflow-artificial*
 TN   Throughflow-entrenched
 TI   Throughflow-intermittent
 BI   Bidirectional-nontidal
 BT   Bidirectional-tidal

*Note: To be used with wetlands connected to streams by ditches.

Other Modifiers (apply at the end of the code as appropriate)

 br   barren
 bv   beaver
 ch   channelized flow
 cl   coastal island (wetland on an island in an estuary or ocean including barrier islands)
 cr   cranberry bog
 dd   drainage divide
 dr   partly drained
 es   freshwater stream or wetland flowing directly into an estuary
 fe   former estuarine wetland
 fg   fragmented
 fm   floating mat
 gd   groundwater-dominated (apply to Water Flow Path only)
 hi   severely human-induced
 hw   headwater
 li   lake island (wetland associated with a lake island)

ow	overwash
pi	pond island border
ri	river island (wetland associated with a river island)
sd	surface water-dominated (apply to Water Flow Path only)
sf	spring-fed
ss	subsurface flow
td	tidally restricted/road
tr	tidally restricted/railroad

(Note: "ho" was formerly used to indicate human-induced outflow brought about by ditch construction; now this is addressed by the water flow path "OA" Outflow-Artificial.)

Codes for Waterbodies

Besides Waterbody Type, waterbodies can be classified by water flow path (for lakes and ponds), estuary hydrologic type (for estuaries), and tidal range types (for estuaries and oceans).

Waterbody Type

RV	River	
	1	low gradient
	a	connecting channel
	b	canal
	2	middle gradient
	a	connecting channel
	3	high gradient
	a	waterfall
	b	riffle
	c	pool
	4	intermittent gradient
	5	tidal gradient
	6	dammed gradient
	a	lock and dammed
	b	run-of-river dammed
	c	other dammed

ST	Stream	
	1	low gradient
	a	connecting channel
	2	middle gradient
	a	connecting channel
	3	high gradient
	a	waterfall
	b	riffle
	c	pool

4		intermittent gradient
5		tidal gradient
6		dammed
a		lock and dammed
b		run-of-river dammed
c		beaver dammed
d		other dammed
7		artificial
a		connecting channel
b		ditch

LK   Lake

1		natural lake (*see also Pond codes for possible specific types*)
a		main body
b		open empbayment
c		semi-enclosed embayment
d		barrier beach lagoon
2		dammed river valley lake
a		reservoir
b		hydropower
c		other
3		other dammed lake
a		former natural
b		artificial
4		other artificial lake

(Consider using a modifier to highlight specific lakes as needed, especially the Great Lakes, e.g., LK1E for Lake Erie or LK2O for Lake Ontario, and Lake Champlain, LK1C)

EY   Estuary

1		drowned river valley estuary
a		open bay (fully exposed)
b		semi-enclosed bay
c		river channel
2		bar-built estuary
a		coastal pond-open
b		coastal pond-seasonally closed
c		coastal pond-intermittently open
d		hypersaline lagoon
3		river-dominated estuary
4		rocky headland bay estuary
a		island protected
5		island protected estuary

6	shoreline bay estuary	
a		open (fully exposed)
b		semi-enclosed
7	tectonic	
a		fault-formed
b		volcanic-formed
8	fjord	
9	other	

Note: If desired, you can also designate river channel (rc), stream channel (sc),and inlet channel (ic) by modifiers. Examples: EY1rc = Drowned River Valley Estuary river channel; EY2ic= Bar-built estuary inlet channel. If not, simply classify all estuarine water as a single type, e.g., EY1 for Drowned River Valley or EY2 for Bar-built Estuary.

OB	Ocean or Bay	
1	open (fully exposed)	
2	semi-protected oceanic bay	
3	atoll lagoon	
4	other reef-protected waters	
5	fjord	

PD	Pond	
1	natural	
a		bog
b		woodland-wetland
c		woodland-dryland
d		prairie-wetland (pothole)
e		prairie-dryland (pothole)
f		playa
g		polygonal
h		sinkhole-woodland
i		sinkhole-prairie
j		Carolina bay
k		pocosin
l		cypress dome
m		vernal-woodland
n		vernal-West Coast
o		interdunal
p		grady
q		floodplain
r		other
2	dammed/impounded	
a		agriculture
a1		cropland
a2		livestock

a3		cranberry
b		aquaculture
b1		catfish
b2		crayfish
c		commercial
c1		commercial-stormwater
d		industrial
d1		industrial-stormwater
d2		industrial-wastewater
e		residential
e1		residential-stormwater
f		sewage treatment
g		golf
h		wildlife management
i		other recreational
o		other
3	excavated	
a		agriculture
a1		cropland
a2		livestock
a3		cranberry
b		aquaculture
b1		catfish
b2		crayfish
c		commercial
c1		commercial-stormwater
d		industrial
d1		industrial-stormwater
d2		industrial-wastewater
e		residential
e1		residential-stormwater
f		sewage treatment
g		golf
h		wildlife management
i		other recreational
j		mining
j1		sand/gravel
j2		coal
o		other
4	beaver	
5	other artificial	

Water Flow Path

IN   Inflow
OU   Outflow
OA   Outflow-artificial*
TH   Throughflow
TA   Throughflow-artificial*
TI   Throughflow-intermittent*
TN   Throughflow-entrenched
BI   Bidirectional-nontidal
IS   Isolated
MI   Microtidal
ME   Mesotidal
MC   Macrotidal

*Note: OA and TA are human-caused by ditches; TI is to be used with throughflow ponds along intermittent streams.

Estuarine Hydrologic Circulation Type

SW   Salt-wedge/river-dominated type
PM   Partially mixed type
HO   Homogeneous/high energy type

Other Modifiers (apply at end of code)

ch   Channelized or Dredged
dv   Diverted
fv   Floating vegetation (on the surface)
lv   Leveed
sv   Submerged vegetation

Section 5. Acknowledgments

The following individuals have assisted in the application of pilot studies which helped improve this classification: Herbert Bergquist, Gabriel DeAlessio, Bobbi Jo McClain, Glenn Smith, Matthew Starr, and John Swords. Others providing input into the refinement of this classification included Dennis Peters, Norm Mangrum, Greg Pipkin, Charlie Storrs, and Elaine Blok. Doug Wilcox provided information on the classification of Great Lakes coastal wetlands. Their contributions have made the system suitable for operational use.

Section 6. References

Ainslie, W.B., R.D. Smith, B.A. Pruitt, T.H. Roberts, E.J. Sparks, L. West, G.L. Godshalk, and M.V. Miller. 1999. A Regional Guidebook for Assessing the Functions of Low Gradient, Riverine Wetlands in Western Kentucky. U.S. Army Engineer Waterways Experiment Station, Vicksburg, MS. Technical Report WRP-DE-17.

Brinson, M.M. 1993. A Hydrogeomorphic Classification for Wetlands. U.S. Army Corps of Engineers, Washington, DC. Wetlands Research Program, Technical Report WRP-DE-4.

Brinson, M.M., F.R. Hauer, L.C. Lee, W.L. Nutter, R.D. Rheinhardt, R.D. Smith, and D. Whigham. 1995. A Guidebook for Application of Hydrogeomorphic Assessments to Riverine Wetlands. U.S. Army Engineer Waterways Experiment Station, Vicksburg, MS. Technical Report WPR-DE-11.

Cowardin, L.M., V. Carter, F.C. Golet, and E.T. LaRoe. 1979. Classification of Wetlands and Deepwater Habitats of the United States. U.S. Fish and Wildlife Service, Washington, DC. FWS/OBS-79/31.

Machung, L. and H.M. Forgione. 2002. A landscape level approach to wetland functional assessment for the New York City water supply watersheds. In: R.W. Tiner (compiler). Watershed-based Wetland Planning and Evaluation. A Collection of Papers from the Wetland Millennium Event (August 6-12, 2000; Quebec City, Quebec, Canada). Distributed by the Association of State Wetland Managers, Inc., Berne, NY. pp. 41-57.

Smith, R.D., A. Ammann, C. Bartoldus, and M.M. Brinson. 1995. An Approach for Assessing Wetland Functions Using Hydrogeomorphic Classification, Reference Wetlands, and Functional Indices. U.S. Army Engineer Waterways Experiment Station, Vicksburg, MS. Technical Report WRP-DE-9.

Smith, R.D. and C.V. Klimas. 2002. A Regional Guidebook for Applying the Hydrogeomorphic Approach to Assessing Wetland Functions of Selected Regional Wetland Subclasses, Yazoo Basin, Lower Mississippi River Alluvial Valley. U.S. Army Engineer Research and Development Center, Vicksburg, MS. Technical Report ERCD/EL TR-02-04. Tiner, R.W. 1995a. A Landscape and Landform Classification for Northeast Wetlands

(Operational Draft). U.S. Fish and Wildlife Service, Ecological Services (NWI), Region 5, Hadley, MA.

Tiner, R.W. 1995b. Piloting a more descriptive NWI. National Wetlands Newsletter 19 (5): 14-16.

Tiner, R.W. 1997a. Adapting the NWI for preliminary assessment of wetland functions. In: The Future of Wetland Assessment: Applying Science through the Hydrogeomorphic Assessment Approach and Other Approaches. Abstracts. The Association of State Wetland Managers, Berne, NY. pp. 105-106.

Tiner, R.W. 1997b. Keys to Landscape Position and Landform Descriptors for U.S. Wetlands (Operational Draft). U.S. Fish and Wildlife Service, Northeast Region, Hadley, MA.

Tiner, R.W. 1999. Wetland Indicators: A Guide to Wetland Identification, Delineation, Classification, and Mapping. Lewis Publishers, CRC Press, Boca Raton, FL.

Tiner, R.W. 2000. Keys to Waterbody Type and Hydrogeomorphic-type Wetland Descriptors for U.S. Waters and Wetlands (Operational Draft). U.S. Fish and Wildlife Service, Northeast Region, Hadley, MA.

Tiner, R., S. Schaller, D. Petersen, K. Snider, K. Ruhlman, and J. Swords. 1999. Wetland Characterization Study and Preliminary Assessment of Wetland Functions for the Casco Bay Watershed, Southern Maine. U.S. Fish and Wildlife Service, Northeast Region. Hadley, MA. With Support from the State of Maine's Wetlands Steering Committee. Prepared for the Maine State Planning Office, Augusta, ME.

Tiner, R., M. Starr, H. Bergquist, and J. Swords. 2000. Watershed-based Wetland Characterization for Maryland's Nanticoke River and Coastal Bays Watersheds: A Preliminary Assessment Report. U.S. Fish and Wildlife Service, Northeast Region, Hadley, MA. Prepared for the Maryland Department of Natural Resources, Annapolis, MD. (see copy on the web at: http://wetlands.fws.gov listed under reports and publications)

Tiner, R.W., H.C. Bergquist, J.Q. Swords, and B.J. McClain. 2001. Watershed-based Wetland Characterization for Delaware's Nanticoke River Watershed: A Preliminary Assessment Report. U.S. Fish and Wildlife Service, Northeast Region, Hadley, MA. Prepared for the Delaware Department of Natural Resources and Environmental Control, Division of Soil and Water Conservation, Dover, DE.

Tiner, R.W. 2002. Enhancing wetland inventory data for watershed-based wetland characterizations and preliminary assessments of wetland functions. In: R.W. Tiner (compiler). Watershed-based Wetland Planning and Evaluation. A Collection of Papers from the Wetland Millennium Event (August 6-12, 2000; Quebec City, Quebec, Canada). Distributed by the Association of State Wetland Managers, Inc., Berne, NY. pp. 17-39. (http://www.aswm.org)

Tiner, R.W. 2003. Correlating Enhanced National Wetlands Inventory Data With Wetland Functions for Watershed Assessments: A Rationale for Northeastern U.S. Wetlands. U.S. Fish and Wildlife Service, National Wetlands Inventory Program, Northeast Region, Hadley, MA.

Section 7. Glossary

Barrier Beach -- a coastal peninsular landform extending from the mainland into the ocean or large embayment or large lake (e.g., Great Lakes), typically providing protection to waters on the backside and allowing the establishment of salt marshes; similar to the barrier island, except connected to the mainland

Barrier Island -- a coastal insular landform, an island typically between the ocean (or possibly the Great Lakes) and the mainland; its presence usually promotes the formation of salt marshes on the backside

Basin -- a depressional (concave) landform; various types are further defined by the absence of a stream (isolated), by the presence of a stream and its position relative to a wetland (throughflow, outflow, inflow), or by its occurrence on a floodplain (floodplain basins include ox-bows and sloughs, for example)

Bay -- a coastal embayment of variable size and shape that is always opens to the sea through an inlet or other features

Carolina Bay -- a wetland formed in a semicircular or egg-shaped basin with a northwest to southeast orientation, found along the Atlantic Coastal Plain from southern New Jersey to Florida, and perhaps most common in Horry County, South Carolina

Channelization -- the act or result of excavating a stream or river channel to increase downstream flow of water or to increase depth for navigational purposes

Channelized -- water flow through a conspicuous drainageway, a stream or a river

Coastal Island - an island in marine and estuarine areas

Coastal Pond - pond and its associated wetlands that form behind a barrier beach and are subjected to varying tidal influence (intermittent to daily); the tidal connection for many coastal ponds has been stabilized by jetties; the ones that are only intermittently connected have low salinities

Connecting Channel - a river or stream that connects two adjacent lakes; lakes are typically close together considering their relative size; it is not any stream that occurs between two lakes in a drainage basin; perhaps the best examples are rivers connecting the Great Lakes, such as the St. Marys River connecting Lake Superior to Lake Huron, Detroit River connecting Lake St. Clair to Lake Erie, and the Niagara River connecting Lake Erie with Lake Ontario

Cypress Dome -- a wetland dominated by bald cypress growing in a basin that may be formed by the collapse of underlying limestone, forest canopy takes on a domed appearance with tallest trees in center and becoming progressively shorter as move toward margins of basin

Delta -- a typically lobed-shaped or fan-shaped landform formed by sedimentation processes at the mouth of a river carrying heavy sediment loads

Ditch B a linear, often shallow, artificial channel created by excavation with intent to improve drainage of or to irrigate adjacent lands

Drained, Partly -- condition where a wetland has been ditched or tiled to lower the ground water table, but the area is still wet long enough and often enough to fall within the range of conditions associated with wetland hydrology

Entrenched -- condition where a stream cuts through a wetland and does not periodically overflow into the wetland; the affected wetland may be a terrene wetland cut by a stream or it could be a lotic wetland along an entrenched stream (the latter would usually have to be identified in the field)

Estuarine -- the landscape of estuaries (salt and brackish tidal waterbodies, such as bays and coastal rivers) including associated wetlands, typically occurring in sheltered or protected areas, not exposed to oceanic currents

Flat -- a relatively level landform; may be a component of a floodplain or the landform of an interfluve

Flatwood -- forest of pines, hardwoods or mixed stands growing on interfluves on the Gulf-Atlantic Coastal Plain, typically with imperfectly drained soils; some flatwoods are wetlands, while others are dryland

Floodplain -- a broad, generally flat landform occurring in a landscape shaped by fluvial or riverine processes; for purposes of this classification limited to the broad plain associated with large river systems subject to periodic flooding (once every 100 years) and typically having alluvial soils; further subdivided into several subcategories: flat (broad, nearly level to gently sloping areas) and basin (depressional features such as ox-bows and sloughs)

Floodplain, active -- floodplain that is typically inundated once every 100 years by natural events

Floodplain, inactive -- floodplain that is no longer flooded once in 100 years due to human-alterations such as leveeing, diking, or altered river flow regimes or to natural processes such as changing river courses

Fringe -- a wetland occurring along a standing or flowing waterbody, i.e., a lake, pond, river, stream, estuary, or ocean, including tidal wetlands that are inundated frequently by tides, nontidal vegetated wetlands that are flooded for most of the growing season, and nonvegetated wetlands that form the banks of these waterbodies (such as cobble-gravel bars along river bends)

Ground Water -- water below ground, held in the soil or underground aquifers

Headland -- the seaward edge of the major continental land mass (North America), commonly called the mainland; not an island

High Gradient -- the fast-flowing segment of a drainage system, typically with no floodplain development; equivalent to the Upper Perennial and Intermittent Subsystems of the Riverine System in Cowardin et al. 1979

Inflow -- water enters; an inflow wetland is one that receives surface water from a stream or other waterbody or from significant surface or ground water from a wetland or waterbody at a higher elevation and has no significant discharge

Interdunal -- occurring between sand dunes, as in interdunal swale wetlands found in dunefields behind ocean and estuarine beaches and in sand plains like the Nebraska Sandhills

Interfluve -- a broad level to imperceptibly depressional poorly drained landform occurring between two drainage systems, most typical of the Coastal Plain

Island -- a landform completely surrounded by water and not a delta; some islands are entirely wetland, while others are uplands with or without a fringe wetland

Isolated -- lacking an apparent surface water connection to other wetlands and waterbodies; typically "geographically isolated" (surrounded by upland - nonhydric soils); may be connected to other wetlands and water via groundwater, but this is not known

Karst -- a limestone region characterized by sinkholes and underground caverns

Kettle -- a glacially formed depression typically created by a block of glacial ice left on the land by a retreating glacier; melting of the ice formed a kettle pond that may be quite deep, with bog vegetation frequently established along its perimeter

Lake Island - an island in a lake

Lentic -- the landscape position associated with large, deep standing waterbodies (such as lakes and reservoirs) and contiguous wetlands formed in the lake basin (excludes seasonal and shallow lakes which are included in the *Terrene* landscape position)

Lotic -- the landscape position associated with flowing water systems (such as rivers, creeks, perennial streams, intermittent streams, and similar waterbodies) and contiguous wetlands

Low Gradient -- the slow-flowing segment of a drainage system, typically with considerable floodplain development; equivalent to the Lower Perennial Subsystem of the Riverine System in Cowardin et al. 1979 plus contiguous wetlands

Marine -- the landscape position (or seascape) associated with the ocean's shoreline

Middle Gradient -- the segment of a drainage system with characteristic intermediate between the high and low gradient reaches, typically with limited floodplain development; equivalent to areas mapped as Riverine Unknown (R5) in the Northeast Region plus contiguous wetlands

Nonchannelized -- water exits through seepage, not through a river or stream channel or ditch

Outflow -- water exits naturally or through artificial means (e.g., ditches); an outflow wetland has water leaving via a stream, seepage, or ditch (artificial) to a wetland or waterbody at a lower elevation; it lacks an inflowing surface water source like an intermittent or perennial stream

Oxbow -- a former mainstem river bend now partly or completely cut off from mainstem

Paludified -- subjected to paludification, the process by which peat moss engulfs terrains of varying elevations due to an excess of water, typically associated with cold, humid climates of northern areas (boreal/arctic regions and fog-shrouded coasts)

Playa -- a type of basin wetland in the Southwest characterized by drastic fluctuations in water levels over the normal wet-dry cycle

Pocosin -- a shrub and/or forested wetland forming on organic soils in interstream divides (interfluves) on the Atlantic Coast Plain from Virginia to Florida, mostly in North Carolina

Pond -- a natural or human-made shallow open waterbody that may be subjected to periodic drawdowns

Prairie Pothole -- a glacially formed basin wetland found in the Upper Midwest especially in the Dakotas, western Minnesota, and Iowa

Reservoir -- a large, deep waterbody formed by a dike or dam created for a water supply for drinking water or agricultural purposes or for flood control, or similar purposes

River Island - an island within a river

Salt Pond -- a coastal embayment of variable size and shape that is periodically and temporarily cut off from the sea by natural accretion processes; some may be kept permanently open by jetties and periodic maintenance dredging

Salt Flat -- a broad expanse of alkaline wetlands associated with arid regions, especially the Great Basin in the western United States

Sinkhole -- a depression formed by the collapse of underlying limestone deposits; may be wetland or nonwetland depending on drainage characteristics

Slope -- a wetland occurring on a slope; various types include those along a sloping stream (fringe), those (paludified) formed by paludification -- the process of bogging or swamping of uplands by peat moss in northern climes (humid and cold), and those not designated as one of the above and typically called seeps

Stream B a natural drainageway that contains flowing water at least seasonally; different stream types: *perennial* where water flows continously in all years except drought or extremely dry years; intermittent where water flows only seasonally in most years; channelized where stream bed has been excavated or dredged

Subsurface Flow -- water leaves via ground water

Surface Water -- water occurring above the ground as in flooded or ponded conditions

Tectonic - changes in the earth's surface caused by landslides, faulting, and volcanic activity

Terrene -- wetlands surrounded or nearly so by uplands and lacking a channelized outlet stream; a stream may enter or exit this type of wetland but it does not flow through it as a channel; includes a variety of wetlands and natural and human-made ponds

Throughflow -- water entering and exiting, passing through; a throughflow wetland receives significant surface or ground water which passes through the wetland and is discharged to a stream, wetland or other waterbody at a lower elevation; throughflow may be perennial, intermittent, or associated with an entrenched stream

Tidal Gradient -- the segment of a drainage basin that is subjected to tidal influence; essentially the freshwater tidal reach of coastal rivers; equivalent to the Tidal Subsystem of the Riverine System in Cowardin et al. 1979 plus contiguous wetlands

Vernal Pool -- a temporarily flooded basin; woodland vernal pools are found in humid temperature regions dominated by trees, these pools are surrounded by upland forests, are usually flooded from winter through mid-summer, and serve as critical breeding grounds for salamanders and woodland frogs; West Coast vernal pools occur in California, Oregon, and Washington on clayey soils, they are important habitats for many rare plants and animals

Appendix B.

Correlating Enhanced NWI Data With Wetland Functions for Watershed Assessments: A Rationale for Northeastern U.S. Wetlands (Tiner 2003b).

CORRELATING ENHANCED NATIONAL WETLANDS INVENTORY DATA
WITH WETLAND FUNCTIONS FOR WATERSHED ASSESSMENTS:
A RATIONALE FOR NORTHEASTERN U.S. WETLANDS

U.S. Fish & Wildlife Service
National Wetlands Inventory Program
Northeast Region
300 Westgate Center Drive
Hadley, MA 01035

Correlating Enhanced National Wetlands Inventory Data
with Wetland Functions for Watershed Assessments:
A Rationale for Northeastern U.S. Wetlands

Ralph W. Tiner
Regional Wetland Coordinator
U.S. Fish & Wildlife Service
Northeast Region
300 Westgate Center Drive
Hadley, MA 01035

October 2003

This publication should be cited as:

Tiner, R.W. 2003. Correlating Enhanced National Wetlands Inventory Data with Wetland
Functions for Watershed Assessments: A Rationale for Northeastern U.S. Wetlands. U.S. Fish
and Wildlife Service, National Wetlands Inventory Program, Region 5, Hadley, MA. 26 pp.

Table of Contents

Background

The U.S. Fish and Wildlife Service has been conducting the National Wetlands Inventory for over 25 years. The NWI Program has produced wetland maps for 91% (78% final) of the lower 48 states, all of Hawaii, and 35% of Alaska. Wetlands are classified according to the Service's official wetland classification system (Cowardin et al. 1979). This classification describes wetlands by ecological system (Marine, Estuarine, Lacustrine, Riverine, and Palustrine), by subsystem (e.g., water depth, exposure to tides), class (vegetative life form or substrate type), subclass, water regimes (hydrology), water chemistry (pH and salinity), and special modifiers (e.g., alterations by humans). The maps have been converted to digital data for 47% of the lower 48 states and 18% of Alaska. The availability of digital data and geographic information system (GIS) technology make it possible to use NWI data for various geospatial analyses.

In the 1990s, the NWI Program for the Northeast Region recognized the potential application of NWI data for watershed assessments, but realized that other attributes would have to be added to the data to facilitate functional analysis. Dr. Mark Brinson had recently developed a hydrogeomorphic (hgm) approach to wetland functional assessment (Brinson 1993a). This approach provided the impetus for developing other attributes to expand the NWI database and make it more useful for functional assessment.

In the mid-1990s, a set of hgm-type descriptors were developed to describe a wetland's landscape position, landform, and water flow path (Tiner 1995, 1996a,b). Use of the initial set of keys for pilot watershed projects lead to a refinement and expansion of the keys in subsequent years (Tiner 1997a, 2000, 2002, 2003). These projects were watershed characterizations that included a preliminary assessment of wetland functions as a main component or the prime component of the study. The reports addressed the following watersheds: Casco Bay (Maine; Tiner et al. 1999), Nanticoke River (Maryland and Delaware; Tiner et al. 2000, 2001), Coastal Bays (Maryland; Tiner et al. 2000), and Cannonsville and Neversink Reservoirs (New York; Tiner et al. 2002), as well as the Pennsylvania Coastal Zone (Tiner and DeAlessio 2002).

In conducting these studies, we worked with local and regional wetland experts to develop correlations between wetland characteristics recorded in the database and wetland functions (see Acknowledgments for listing). The correlations reflect our best approximation of what types of wetlands are likely to perform certain functions at significant levels based on the characteristics we have in the wetland database. Conducting wetland assessments in other areas, especially in arid, semiarid, and tropical regions, may identify other wetlands that need to be added to the significance list for various functions.

Limitations of the Preliminary Wetland Functional Assessment

Source data are a primary limiting factor. NWI digital data are used as the foundation for these assessments. In some cases, the NWI data are derived by updating more detailed state wetland data. Nonetheless, all wetland mapping has limitations due to scale, photo quality, date of the survey, and the difficulty of photointerpreting certain wetland types (especially evergreen forested wetlands and drier-end wetlands; see Tiner 1997c, 1999 for details).

Recognizing source data limitations, it is equally important to understand that this type of functional assessment is a preliminary one based on wetland characteristics interpreted through remote sensing and using the best professional judgment of various specialists to develop correlations between wetland characteristics in the database and wetland functions. Also, no attempt is made to produce a more qualitative ranking for each function or for each wetland based on multiple functions as this would require more input from others and more data, well beyond the scope of this type of evaluation. For a technical review of wetland functions, see Mitsch and Gosselink (2000) and for a broad overview, see Tiner (1998).

Functional assessment of wetlands can involve many parameters. Typically such assessments have been done in the field on a case-by-case basis, considering observed features relative to those required to perform certain functions or by actual measurement of performance. The preliminary assessments based on remotely sensed information do not seek to replace the need for field evaluations since they represent the ultimate assessment of the functions for individual wetlands. Yet, for a watershed analysis, basin-wide field-derived assessments are not practical, cost-effective, or even possible given access considerations. For watershed planning purposes, a more generalized assessment (level 1 assessment) is worthwhile for targeting wetlands that may provide certain functions, especially for those functions dependent on landscape position, landform, hydrologic processes, and vegetative life form. Subsequently, these results can be field-verified when it comes to actually evaluating particular wetlands for acquisition purposes (e.g., for conserving biodiversity or for preserving flood storage capacity) or for project impact assessment. Current aerial photography may also be examined to aid in further evaluations (e.g., condition of wetland/stream buffers or adjacent land use) that can supplement the preliminary assessment.

The functional assessment approach -"Watershed-based Preliminary Assessment of Wetland Functions" (W-PAWF) - applies general knowledge about wetlands and their functions to develop a watershed overview that highlights possible wetlands of significance in terms of performance of various functions. To accomplish this objective, the relationships between wetlands and various functions are simplified into a set of practical criteria or observable characteristics. Such assessments may be further expanded to consider the condition of the associated waterbody and the neighboring upland or to evaluate the opportunity a wetland has to perform a particular function or service to society, for example.

W-PAWF usually does not account for the opportunity that a wetland has to provide a function resulting from a certain land-use practice upstream or the presence of certain structures or land-uses downstream. For example, two wetlands of equal size and like vegetation may be in the right landscape position to retain sediments. One, however, may be downstream of a land-clearing operation that has generated considerable suspended sediments in the water column, while the other is downstream from an undisturbed forest. The former should be actively performing sediment trapping in a major way, whereas the latter is not. Yet if land-clearing takes place in the latter area, the second wetland will likely trap sediments as well as the first wetland. The entire analysis typically tends to ignore opportunity since such opportunity may have occurred in the past or may occur in the future and the wetland is there to perform this service at higher levels when necessary.

W-PAWF also does not consider the condition of the adjacent upland (e.g., level of disturbance) or the actual water quality of the associated waterbody that may be regarded as important metrics for assessing the health of individual wetlands. Collection and analysis of these data may be done as a followup investigation, where desired.

It is important re-emphasize that the preliminary assessment does not obviate the need for more detailed assessments of the various functions. This type of assessment should be viewed as a starting point for more rigorous assessments, since it attempts to cull out wetlands that may likely provide significant functions based on generally accepted principles and the source information used for this analysis. This assessment is most useful for regional or watershed planning purposes. For site-specific evaluations, additional work will be required, especially field verification and collection of site-specific data for potential functions (e.g., following the HGM assessment approach as described by Brinson 1993a or other onsite evaluation procedures). This is particularly true for assessments of fish and wildlife habitats and biodiversity. Other sources of data may exist to help refine some of the findings of this report (e.g., state natural heritage data). Additional modeling could be done, for example, to identify habitats of likely significance to individual species of animals based on their specific life history requirements (see U.S. Fish and Wildlife Service 2003 for Gulf of Maine habitat analysis).

Also note that the criteria used for the correlations were based on regional application of the Service's wetland classification (Cowardin et al. 1979). Regional applications of this system may differ slightly depending on regional priorities, level of field effort, and knowledge of wetland ecology. Use of the correlations in other regions of the country therefore may require some adjustment based on these considerations.

Through this analysis, numerous wetlands are predicted to perform a given function at a significant level presumably important to a watershed's ability to provide that function. "Significance" is a relative term and is used in this analysis to identify wetlands that are likely to perform a given function at a level above that of wetlands not designated. It is also emphasized that the assessment is limited to wetlands (i.e., areas classified as wetlands on NWI maps or similar sources). Deepwater habitats and streams were not included in the assessment, although their inherent value to wetlands and many wetland-dependent organisms is apparent.

Rationale for Preliminary Functional Assessments

A maximum of ten functions may be evaluated: 1) surface water detention, 2) coastal storm surge detention, 3) streamflow maintenance, 4) nutrient transformation, 5) sediment and other particulate retention, 6) shoreline stabilization, 7) provision of fish and shellfish habitat, 8) provision of waterfowl and waterbird habitat, 9) provision of other wildlife habitat, and 10) conservation of biodiversity. The criteria used for identifying wetlands of significance for these functions using the digital wetland database are discussed below. The criteria were initially developed by the author of this report based on his knowledge of wetland characteristics and functions. The draft criteria were then reviewed and modified for the subject watersheds based on comments from wetland specialists working on specific watersheds in four Northeast states (Maine, New York, Delaware, and Maryland). (Note: Criteria may need to be modified for other regions of the country, although many are universally applicable.)

In developing a protocol for designating wetlands of potential significance, wetland size was generally disregarded from the criteria, with few exceptions (i.e., other wildlife habitat and biodiversity functions). This approach was followed because it was felt that individual agencies and organizations using the digital database and charged with setting priorities should make the decision on appropriate size criteria as a means of limiting the number of priority wetlands, if necessary. There is no science-based size limit to establish significance for any function. However, it is obvious that, all things being equal, a larger wetland will have a higher capacity to perform a given function than a smaller one of the same type. The W-PAWF approach is intended to produce a more expansive characterization of wetlands and their likely functions and not to develop a rapid assessment method for ranking wetlands for acquisition, protection, or other purposes.

The criteria for identifying different levels of potential significance can be modified in the future based on additional peer review, application to other watersheds and regions, and field evaluation. The proposed criteria are designed for wetlands in the Northeast, but many, if not most, should be relevant nationwide. Some of the criteria, especially those addressing fish and wildlife habitat, will need to be re-examined for individual watersheds, particularly when this approach is applied to other regions of the country. Note that palustrine farmed wetlands have not been identified as being significant for any function in the Northeast. Since they are tilled cropland or cultivated cranberry bogs, farmed wetlands were viewed as severely degraded wetlands that perform the specified functions at minimal levels. Consequently, they represented sites where substantial gains in wetland functions may be achieved through restoration projects. In other parts of the country, farmed wetlands may perform some wetland functions at significant levels (e.g., farmed pothole wetlands in the Midwest or diked former tidelands in the Sacramento River valley - important waterfowl habitat).

4

Surface Water Detention

This function is important for reducing downstream flooding and lowering flood heights, both of which aid in minimizing property damage and personal injury from such events. In a landmark study on the relationships between wetlands and flooding at the watershed scale, Novitzki (1979) found that watersheds with 40 percent coverage by lakes and wetlands had significantly reduced flood flows -- lowered by as much as 80 percent -- compared to similar watersheds with no or few lakes and wetlands in Wisconsin. Floodplain wetlands, other lotic wetlands (basin and flat types), estuarine fringe wetlands along coastal rivers, and estuarine island wetlands in these rivers provide this function at significant levels. At the present time, estuarine and marine rocky shores are rated as high for this function, since they are usually narrow habitats and/or intermixed with tidal flats. Perhaps this function should be limited to non-estuarine habitats, with the water storage function of estuarine wetlands listed under coastal storm surge detention and shoreline stabilization. Presently, estuarine and marine wetlands are recognized as important areas for storing surface water, recognizing that it is tidal water that ebbs and flows.

Wetlands dominated by trees and/or dense stands of shrubs could be deemed to provide a higher level of this function than emergent wetlands, since woody vegetation (with higher frictional resistance) may further aid in flood desynchronization. However, emergent wetlands along waterways provide significant flood storage, so no distinction is made regarding the type of vegetative cover. Floodplain width could also be an important factor in evaluating the significance of performance of this function by individual wetlands (e.g., for acquisition or strengthened protection), but there is no scientifically based criterion for establishing a significance threshold based on size.

Interfluve wetlands and drier-end wetlands (e.g., Lotic Flats) are rated as having moderate potential. While Interfluve basins hold more water than Interfluve flats, no distinction was made since they represent a single system that tends to be dominated by flats. Wetland size was not considered, but it is obvious that size should make a difference in the amount of water stored. Others interested in prioritizing wetlands for acquisition or protection may wish to identify a minimum threshold for importance for this function or develop other criteria for prioritization (e.g., treat small interfluve flats differently from small interfluve basins).

For this function, the following correlations are used:

High	Estuarine Fringe, Estuarine Basin, Estuarine Island, Lentic Basin, Lentic Fringe, Lentic Island (basin and fringe), Lentic Flat associated with reservoirs and flood control dams, Lotic Basin, Lotic Floodplain, Lotic Fringe, Lotic Island associated with Floodplain area, Lotic Island basin, Marine Fringe, Marine Island, Ponds Throughflow (in-stream) and associated Fringe and Basin wetlands, Ponds Bidirectional and associated wetlands, Terrene Throughflow Basin

Moderate	Lotic Flat, Lotic Island flat, Lentic Flat, Terrene Interfluve, Other Terrene Basins, Other Ponds and associated wetlands (excluding sewage treatment ponds and similar waters)

Coastal Storm Surge Detention

This function is listed separately from Surface Water Detention to highlight the importance of tidal wetlands at storing tidal waters brought into estuaries by storms (e.g., Nor'easters, tropical storms, and hurricanes). Estuarine and freshwater tidal wetlands are important areas for temporary storage of this water. At the present time, estuarine and marine rocky shores that are fringe types are rated as high for this function, since they are usually narrow habitats and/or intermixed with tidal flats. Some nontidal wetlands contiguous to these wetlands (e.g., low-lying terrene outflow basins - flatwoods) may also provide this function, but it was not possible to predict the extent of such storage as this depends on storm intensity and frequency.

For this function, the following correlations are used:

High	Estuarine Basin, Estuarine Fringe, Estuarine Island, Lotic Tidal Fringe, Lotic Tidal Island, Lotic Tidal Floodplain, Marine Fringe

Streamflow Maintenance

Many wetlands are sources of groundwater discharge and some may be in a position to sustain streamflow in the watershed. Such wetlands are critically important for supporting aquatic life in streams. All wetlands classified as headwater wetlands are important for streamflow (e.g, Terrene headwater wetlands, by definition, are sources of streams). These wetlands include lotic wetlands along 1st-order streams and lentic wetlands associated with outflow lakes. Wetlands along 2nd-order streams in mountainous areas may be classified as headwater wetlands as they probably are sites of groundwater discharge. Ditched headwater wetlands are rated as "Moderate," since this alteration typically results in faster release of water, thereby reducing the period of outflow. Outflow from groundwater-fed wetlands (lacking a stream) may discharge directly into streams and thereby contribute substantial quantities of water for sustaining baseflows. These wetlands were rated as "Moderate" for this function. Lakes may also be important regulators of streamflow, so lentic wetlands may be designated as significant to streamflow, with those in headwater positions being rated "High" and others as "Moderate."

Floodplain wetlands are known to store water in the form of bank storage, later releasing this water to maintain baseflows (Whiting 1998). Among several key factors affecting bank storage are porosity and permeability of the bank material, the width of the floodplain, and the hydraulic gradient (steepness of the water table). The wider the floodplain, the more bank storage given the same soils. Gravel floodplains drain in days, sandy floodplains in a few weeks to a few years, silty floodplains in years, and clayey floodplains in decades. In good water years, wide sandy floodplains may help maintain baseflows. Despite these differences, the W-PAWF assessment treats all floodplain wetlands similarly, since it is based on remote sensing and does not include soil examinations.

6

For this function, the following correlations are used:

High   Nonditched Headwater Wetlands (Terrene, Lotic, and
            Lentic), Headwater Ponds and Lakes (classified as
            PUB...on NWI) (Note: Lotic Stream Basin or Floodplain
            basin Wetlands along 2nd order streams should also be
            rated high; possibly expand to 3rd order strreams in hilly or
            mountainous terrain.)

Moderate   Ditched Headwater Wetlands (Terrene, Lotic, and Lentic),
            Lotic (Nontidal) Floodplain, Throughflow Ponds and Lakes
            (classified as PUB...on NWI) and their associated wetlands,
            Terrene Outflow Wetlands (associated with streams not
            major rivers), Outflow Ponds and Lakes (classified as
            PUB...on NWI)

Special Note: All these wetlands should be considered to also be important for fish and shellfish as they are vital to sustaining streamflow necessary for the survival of these aquatic organisms.

Nutrient Transformation

All wetlands recycle nutrients, but those having a fluctuating water table are best able to recycle nitrogen and other nutrients. Vegetation slows the flow of water causing deposition of mineral and organic particles with adsorbed nutrients (nitrogen and phosphorus), whereas hydric soils are the places where chemical transformations occur (Carter 1996). Microbial action in the soil is the driving force behind chemical transformations in wetlands. Microbes need a food source -- organic matter -- to survive, so wetlands with high amounts of organic matter should have an abundance of microflora to perform the nutrient cycling function. Wetlands are so effective at filtering and transforming nutrients that artificial wetlands are constructed for water quality renovation (e.g., Hammer 1992). Natural wetlands performing this function help improve local water quality of streams and other watercourses.

Numerous studies have demonstrated the importance of wetlands in denitrification. Simmons et al. (1992) found high nitrate removal (greater than 80%) from groundwater during both the growing season and dormant season in Rhode Island streamside (lotic) wetlands. Groundwater temperatures throughout the dormant season were between 6.5 and 8.0 degrees C, so microbial activity was not limited by temperature. Even the nearby upland, especially transitional areas with somewhat poorly drained soils, experienced an increase in nitrogen removal during the dormant season. This was attributed to a seasonal rise in the water table that exposed the upper portion of the groundwater to soil with more organic matter (nearer the ground surface), thereby supporting microbial activity and denitrification. Riparian forests dominated by wetlands have a greater proportion of groundwater (with nitrate) moving within the biologically active zone of the soil that makes nitrate susceptible to uptake by plants and microbes (Nelson et al. 1995). Riparian forests on well-drained soils are much less effective at removing nitrate. In a Rhode Island study, Nelson et al. (1995) found that November had the highest nitrate removal rate due to the highest water tables in the poorly drained soils, while June experienced the lowest removal rate when the deepest water table levels occurred. Similar results can be expected to occur elsewhere. For bottomland hardwood wetlands, DeLaune et al. (1996) reported decreases in nitrate from 59-82 percent after 40 days of flooding wetland soil cores taken from the Cache River floodplain in Arkansas. Moreover, they surmised that denitrification in these soils appeared to be carbon-limited: increased denitrification took place in soils with more organic matter in the surface layer.

Nitrogen fixation is accomplished in wetlands by microbial-driven reduction processes that convert nitrate to nitrogen gas. Nitrogen removal rates for freshwater wetlands are very high (averaging from 20-80 grams/square meter) (Bowden 1987). The following information comes from a review paper on this topic by Buresh et al. (1980). Nitrogen fixation has been attributed to blue-green algae in the photic zone at the soil-water interface and to heterotrophic bacteria associated with plant roots. In working with rice, Matsuguchi (1979) believed that the significance of heterotrophic fixation in the soil layer beyond the roots has been underrated and presented data showing that such zones were the most important sites for nitrogen fixation in a Japanese rice field. This conclusion was further supported by Wada et al. (1978). Higher fixation rates have been found in the rhizosphere of wetland plants than in dryland plants.

Phosphorus removal is largely done by plant uptake (Patrick, undated manuscript). Wetlands that accumulate peat have a great capacity for phosphorus removal. Wetland drainage can, therefore, change a wetland from a phosphorus sink to a phosphorus source. This is a significant cause of water quality degradation in many areas of the world including the United States, where wetlands are drained for agricultural production. Hydric soils with significant clay constituents fix phosphorus due to its interaction with clay and inorganic colloids. Reduced soils have more sorption sites than oxidized soils (Patrick and Khalid 1974), while the latter soils have stronger bonding energy and adsorb phosphorus more tightly.

From the water quality standpoint, wetlands associated with watercourses are probably the most noteworthy. Numerous studies have found that forested wetlands along rivers and streams ("riparian forested wetlands") are important for nutrient retention and sedimentation during floods (Whigham et al. 1988; Yarbro et al. 1984; Simpson et al. 1983; Peterjohn and Correll 1982). This function by forested riparian wetlands is especially important in agricultural areas. Brinson (1993b) suggests that riparian wetlands along low-order streams may be more important than those along higher order streams.

Wetlands with seasonally flooded and wetter water regimes (including tidal regimes - seasonally flooded-tidal, irregularly flooded, and regularly flooded) are identified as having potential to recycle nutrients at high levels of performance. The soils of these wetlands should have substantial amounts of organic matter near the surface that promote microbial activity and denitrification when wet. Based on field observations, in general, there is a positive correlation between the amount of organic matter and the degree of wetness as reflected by the NWI's water regime classification in wetlands of the Nanticoke River watershed in Delaware (Amy Jacobs, pers. comm. 2003). Periodically flooded soils also retain sediments and their adsorbed nutrients.

Seasonally saturated wetlands are also rated as having high potential for this function. Most the

8

the groundwater flux from uplands to surface waters occurs in the non-growing season in the Northeast and reasonable denitrification rates occur in spring and fall making sites that are wet during these times important for nutrient retention (Art Gold, pers. comm. 2003). Permanently saturated wetlands in nutrient-rich sites should also be rated as high for this function, whereas wetlands with this hydrology in nutrient-poor areas are rated as moderate. The latter types are nutrient-deficient habitats, yet they may have considerable potential for nutrient uptake should more nutrients become available due to land use practices.

Wetlands with a temporarily flooded water regime including those in tidal environments (temporarily flooded-tidal) are identified as having a moderate potential for performing this function. Vegetated wetlands with a seasonally saturated water regime are also considered as moderate, since they are usually wet longer during the non-growing season and for shorter periods during the growing season.

Drainage through ditches or tiles can significantly reduce nutrient transformation by lowering the water table below the zone of highest biological activity (Art Gold, pers. comm. 2003). Partly drained wetlands that are listed as having wetter water regimes (i.e., C, E and F) should still perform this function significantly (i.e., like their nondrained counterparts) since this function appears positively correlated with water regime. Drained wetlands on the drier-end of the soil moisture gradient (i.e., A and B water regimes) likely perform this function to a less degree and are therefore rated as having moderate potential.

For this function, correlations are the following:

High	Vegetated wetlands (and mixes with nonvegetated wetlands or unconsolidated bottom; even where nonvegetated predominates) with seasonally flooded (C), seasonally flooded/saturated (E), semipermanently flooded (F), semipermanently flooded-tidal (T), seasonally flooded-tidal (R), irregularly flooded (P), regularly flooded (N), and permanently flooded (H or L) water regimes, vegetated wetlands with <u>permanently saturated</u> water regime (B; *not on the coastal plain or glaciolacustrine plains*).
Moderate	Vegetated wetlands with <u>seasonally saturated</u> (B *on the coastal plain and on glaciolacustrine plains*, e.g., Great Lakes Plain in western New York), temporarily flooded (A) or temporarily flooded-tidal (S) water regimes

Retention of Sediments and Other Particulates

Many wetlands owe their existence to being located in areas of sediment deposition. This is especially true for floodplain and estuarine wetlands. This function supports water quality maintenance by capturing sediments with bonded nutrients or heavy metals (as in and downstream of urban areas). Estuarine and floodplain wetlands plus lotic (streamside) and lentic (lakeshore) fringe and basin wetlands including lotic (in-stream) ponds are likely to trap and retain sediments and particulates at significant levels. Terrene throughflow basins should function similarly. Vegetated wetlands will likely favor sedimentation over nonvegetated wetlands and are therefore rated higher. Lotic flat wetlands are flooded only for brief periods and less frequently than the wetlands listed above due to their elevation; they are classified as having moderate potential for sediment retention. Throughflow (in-stream) ponds are rated as "High," since they occur within the stream network. Other ponds may be locally significant in retaining such materials, and are also designated as "Moderate." Interfluve flats are not rated as potentially significant because they are level landscapes that do not appear to accumulate substantial amounts of sediment from surrounding areas, whereas Interfluve basins are depressional landscapes that likely collect sediments. The latter wetlands were rated as having moderate potential. Bogs and rocky shores are not considered significant sites for sediment retention and are therefore excluded from the list. Wetlands that are not flooded (e.g., seasonally saturated flatwoods) are also not considered to perform this function at significant levels.

For this function, the following correlations are used:

High	Estuarine Basin (vegetated), Estuarine Fringe (vegetated excluding rocky shores), Estuarine Island (vegetated), Lentic Basin, Lentic Fringe (vegetated only), Lentic Island (vegetated) Lotic Basin, Lotic Floodplain, Lotic Fringe (vegetated), Lotic Island (vegetated), Throughflow Ponds and Lakes (in-stream; designated as PUB... on NWI) and associated vegetated wetlands, Bidirectional Ponds and associated vegetated wetlands, Terrene Throughflow Basin and Interfluve Basin
Moderate	Estuarine Basin (nonvegetated), Estuarine Fringe (nonvegetated excluding rocky shore), Estuarine Island (nonvegetated, excluding rocky shore), Lotic Island (nonvegetated), Lotic Flat (excluding bogs), Lotic Tidal Fringe (nonvegetated), Lentic Flat, Marine Fringe (excluding rocky shore), Marine Island (excluding rocky shore), Other Terrene Basins (excluding bogs), Other Terrene Interfluve Basins, Terrene wetlands associated with ponds (excluding excavated ponds; also excluding bogs and slope wetlands), Other Ponds and Lakes (classified as PUB... on NWI) and associated wetlands (excluding bogs and slope wetlands) *(Note: Users might want to consider removing certain types of ponds from this category, such as ponds with minimal watersheds - possibly gravel pit ponds, impoundments completely surrounded by dikes, and dug-out ponds with little surface water inflow.)*

Shoreline Stabilization

Vegetated wetlands along all waterbodies (e.g., estuaries, lakes, rivers, and streams) provide this function. Vegetation stabilizes the soil or substrate and diminishes wave action, thereby reducing shoreline erosion potential. There is less wave or erosive action along pond shores, so vegetated shoreline wetlands along ponds are designated as "Moderate." Marine and estuarine rocky shores form stable shorelines in several parts of the country. Consequently, they are rated as "High" for this function, except where these wetland types are islands that are inundated completely at times. In the latter situation, they are not shoreline features fringing an upland.

For this function, the following correlations are used:

High   Estuarine wetlands (vegetated except island types), Estuarine
              Rocky Shore (excluding island types), Marine Rocky Shore
              (excluding island types), Lotic wetlands (vegetated except island
              and isolated types), Lentic wetlands (vegetated except island types)

Moderate   Terrene vegetated wetlands associated with ponds (e.g., Fringe-
              pond, Flat-pond, and Basin-pond)

Provision of Fish and Shellfish Habitat[4]

The assessment of potential habitat for fish and shellfish is based on generalities that could be refined for particular species of interest by others at a later date if desireable. Regional and local variations will need to be accounted for on a watershed-by-watershed basis. The criteria selected below are useful for the Northeast and many may be applicable nationwide, but they should be re-examined for each project watershed to ensure accuracy and completeness. Although focused on fish and shellfish, wetlands identified as significant for these species are likely also significant for other aquatic-dependent species such as muskrat, turtles, and numerous frogs.

For tidal areas, the assessment emphasizes palustrine and riverine tidal emergent wetlands, unconsolidated shores (tidal flats), and estuarine wetlands. For nontidal regions, palustrine aquatic beds and semipermanently flooded wetlands are ranked higher than seasonally flooded types due to the longer duration of surface water. Palustrine forested wetlands along streams (lotic stream wetlands) are recognized as important for maintaining fish and shellfish habitat since their canopies help moderate water temperatures and their leaf litter provides food for aquatic organisms (e.g., aquatic invertebrates) that sustain juvenile and some adult fishes. Many ponds (excluding wastewater ponds, for example) and the shallow marsh-open water zone of impoundments are identified as wetlands having moderate potential for fish and shellfish habitat. Those associated with semipermanently flooded wetlands were listed as "High" since they are important nursery grounds and feeding grounds for adults of some species.

Other wetlands providing significant fish habitat may exist, but are not identified. Such wetlands

---

[4] This assessment is focused on wetlands, not deepwater habitats, hence the exclusion of the latter from this analysis, despite widespread recognition that rivers, streams, ponds, and impoundments are the primary habitats for fish and shellfish.

may be identified based on actual observations or culled out from site-specific fisheries information that may be available from other sources. Moreover, all wetlands that are significant for the streamflow maintenance function could be considered vital to sustaining the watershed's ability to provide in-stream fish and shellfish habitat. While these wetlands may not be providing significant fish and shellfish habitat themselves, they support base flows essential to keeping water in streams for aquatic life. Terrene outflow wetlands and Lotic basin wetlands along low order streams (e.g., orders 1-2 in Coastal Plain and 1-3 in hilly or mountainous terrain) often discharge cool groundwater to streams which keeps these streams cooler in summer. Such wetlands are important for providing summer refuges for trout and other coldwater species, especially in warm climate regions (Francis Brautigam, pers. comm. 2003). Other wetlands along waterbodies provide food that supports aquatic organisms that are an important part of the diet of juvenile and some adult fishes.

For this function, the following correlations are used:

High	Estuarine Emergent Wetland (including mixtures with other types where Emergent is the dominant class), Estuarine Unconsolidated Shore, Estuarine Intertidal Reef, Estuarine Aquatic Bed, Estuarine Intertidal Rocky Shore, Lacustrine Semipermanently Flooded (excluding wetlands along intermittent streams), Lacustrine Littoral Aquatic Bed, Lacustrine Littoral Unconsolidated Bottom/Vegetated Wetland, Lacustrine Littoral Vegetated Wetland with a Permanently Flooded water regime, Marine Aquatic Bed, Marine Intertidal Rocky Shore, Marine Intertidal Unconsolidated Shore, Marine Intertidal Reef, Palustrine Semipermanently Flooded (excluding wetlands along intermittent streams; *must be contiguous with a permanent waterbody* such as PUBH, L1UBH, or R2/R3UBH), Palustrine Aquatic Bed, Palustrine Unconsolidated Bottom/Vegetated Wetland, Palustrine Vegetated Wetland with a Permanently Flooded water regime, Palustrine Tidal Emergent Wetland with N, R, T, or L water regimes (excluding "R" wetlands where EM5 is only dominant), Ponds (PUBH.. on NWI; not PUBF) associated with Semipermanently Flooded Vegetated Wetland, Riverine Tidal Emergent Wetland, Riverine Tidal Unconsolidated Shore (excluding those with an "S" water regime)
Moderate	Estuarine Wetlands where Forested or Scrub-Shrub Wetland is mixed with Emergent Wetland, Palustrine Tidal Forested or Scrub-Shrub Wetland mixed with Emergent Wetland having a R or T water regime, Lentic wetlands that are PEM1E, Lotic River or Stream wetlands that are PEM1E (including mixtures with Scrub-Shrub or Forested wetlands), Semipermanently flooded <u>Phragmites</u> wetlands (PEM5F) where contiguous with a permanent waterbody, Other Ponds and associated Fringe wetlands (i.e., Terrene Fringe-pond) (excluding industrial, stormwater

12

treatment/detention, similar ponds in highly disturbed landscapes, and ponds with K and F water regimes)

Important for
Stream
Shading   Lotic Stream wetlands that are Palustrine Forested or Scrub-shrub wetlands (includes mixes where one of these types predominates; excluding those along intermittent streams; also excluding shrub bogs) (*Note that although forested wetlands are designated as important for stream shading, forested upland provide similar functions*)

Local   Lake Champlain example: Seasonally flooded Lentic wetlands (along Lake Champlain - important spawning areas in spring)

Provision of Waterfowl and Waterbird Habitat

Wetlands designated as important for waterfowl (e.g., ducks, geese, mergansers, and loons) and waterbirds (e.g., wading birds, shorebirds, rails, marsh wrens, and red-winged blackbirds) are generally those used for nesting, reproduction, or feeding. The emphasis is on the wetter wetlands and ones that are frequently flooded for long periods. The criteria for selection should be re-examined for each watershed as there may be regional and local differences in habitat requirements that need to be accounted for. The criteria listed below should, however, be useful for most of the country.

The selected wetlands include estuarine wetlands (vegetated or not), riverine emergent wetlands, estuarine and riverine unconsolidated shores (excluding temporary flooded-tidal), palustrine tidal and riverine tidal emergent wetlands (including emergent/shrub mixtures), semipermanently flooded wetlands, mixed open water-emergent wetlands (palustrine and lacustrine), and aquatic beds. Marine rocky shores are rated as having "High" since sea ducks, mergansers, and loons feed extensively in such areas (George Haas, pers. comm. 2003). Phragmites-dominated wetlands are listed as "Moderate" when they are contiguous to a permanent waterbody; those that are flooded either regularly flooded (N) in tidal areas or semipermanently flooded (F) in nontidal areas are designated as "High" since they provide excellent escape cover and night roosting cover (George Haas, pers. comm. 2003). For this analysis, palustrine tidal scrub-shrub/emergent wetlands and tidal forested/emergent wetlands were designated as having moderate significance for these birds. Similar mixed wetlands dominated by emergent species, however, are listed as having high significance, since the emergents typically represent wetter conditions. Ponds were considered to have moderate potential for providing waterfowl and waterbird habitat.[5] Phragmites-dominated wetlands were listed as having moderate potential for they receive some use by waterfowl and waterbirds.

---

[5]Ponds on wildlife management areas (e.g., refuges) should be considered to be of high significance due to their management. Since we do not presently have the location of refuges recorded in our digital database, these ponds may not be separated from the rest of the ponds. Hence, all ponds except industrial, commercial, stormwater detention, wastewater treatment, and similar ponds, are designated as having moderate potential for this function.

Other wetlands that may be significant principally for wood duck are identified. Since wooded streams are particularly important for them, seasonally flooded lotic wetlands that are forested or mixtures of trees and shrubs (excluding those along intermittent streams) are designated as wetlands with significant potential for use by this species. Similar seasonally flooded-tidal wetlands bordering oligohaline estuarine wetlands may also be important for wood duck as well as for providing shelter from winter storms for overwintering black ducks. Recognize that wetlands listed as having high potential for waterfowl and waterbird habitat also include some types important to wood ducks (e.g., semipermanently flooded lotic shrub/emergent wetlands); their value to wood ducks has not been highlighted given that they were already designated as having high potential for waterfowl and waterbirds.

Seasonally flooded emergent wetlands (including mixtures with shrubs) were not designated as potentially significant for waterfowl and waterbirds. Field checking of these types may reveal that some are freshwater marshes that provide significant habitat; they should then be added to database as wetlands of significance for this function. Although palustrine forested wetlands along freshwater tidal rivers and streams were designated as important for wood duck, similar wetlands behind estuarine wetlands (salt marshes, not oligohaline marshes) were not identified as significant. These wetlands need further evaluation by local waterfowl experts as we recognize that forested wetlands provide important shelter for overwintering black ducks during coastal storm events, but are uncertain as to the role played by this subset of forested wetlands.

For this function, the following correlations were used:

High   Estuarine Aquatic Bed, Estuarine Emergent wetlands (excluding Phragmites-dominated wetlands; including mixtures with other vegetated types, e.g., EM/SS), Estuarine Unconsolidated Shore (except S water regime), Estuarine Intertidal Reef, Lacustrine Semipermanently Flooded, Lacustrine Littoral Aquatic Bed, Lacustrine Littoral Vegetated wetlands with an H water regime, Lacustrine Unconsolidated Shores (F, E, or C water regimes; mudflats), Marine Aquatic Bed, Marine Intertidal Reef, Marine Unconsolidated Shore, Marine Rocky Shores, Palustrine Semipermanently Flooded and Semipermanently Flooded-Tidal (excluding Phragmites stands, but including mixtures containing this species - EM5), Palustrine Aquatic Bed, Palustrine Vegetated wetlands with a H water regime, Palustrine Unconsolidated Shores (F, E, or C water regimes; mudflats), Seasonally Flooded/Saturated Palustrine wetlands impounded or beaver-influenced (all vegetation types [except PEM5Eh and PEM5Eb] and associated PUB waters), Lotic River or Stream wetlands that are PEM1E (including mixtures with Scrub-Shrub or Forested wetlands), Ponds associated with Semipermanently Flooded Vegetated wetlands,

Palustrine Tidal Emergent wetlands (PEM1R and PEM1T and mixes with other EM and with SS and FO; excluding wetlands where EM5 is the only EM), Riverine Tidal Emergent wetlands, Riverine Tidal Unconsolidated Shores (except with S water regime), Ponds associated with all of the above wetland types

Moderate   Phragmites wetlands that are Seasonally Flooded/Saturated and wetter (PEM5E; PEM5F; PEM5H, and PEM5R) *and* contiguous with a waterbody, Phragmites-dominated Estuarine Emergent wetlands *and* contiguous to a waterbody, Seasonally Flooded-Tidal Palustrine Wetland where EM is the subordinate mixed class (e.g., PFO1/EM1R), Other Lacustrine Littoral Unconsolidated Bottom, Other Palustrine Unconsolidated Bottom (excluding industrial, commercial, stormwater detention, wastewater treatment, and similar ponds), Palustrine Emergent wetlands (including mixtures with Scrub-shrub) that are Seasonally Flooded and associated with permanently flooded waterbodies

Significant for
Wood Duck   Lotic wetlands (excluding those along intermittent streams) that are Forested or Scrub-shrub or mixtures of these types with C, E, F, R, or H water regime; Lotic wetlands that are mixed Forested/Emergent or Unconsolidated Bottom/Forested with a E, F, R, or H water regime; Palustrine Tidal Forested or Scrub-shrub wetlands (and mixes with other types like the Lotic types) in estuarine reach with R or L water regime

Provision of Other Wildlife Habitat

The provision of other wildlife habitat by wetlands was evaluated in general terms. Species-specific habitat requirements were not considered. The criteria listed below are designed for the Northeast and many should be useful nationwide, but habitat requirements for regional and local wildlife need to be considered on a watershed-by-watershed basis for best results.

In developing an evaluation method for wildlife habitat in the glaciated Northeast, Golet (1972) designated several types as outstanding wildlife wetlands including: 1) wetlands with rare, restricted, endemic, or relict flora and/or fauna, 2) wetlands with unusually high visual quality and infrequent occurrence, 3) wetlands with flora and fauna at the limits of their range, 4) wetlands with several seral stages of hydrarch succession, and 5) wetlands used by great numbers of migratory waterfowl, shorebirds, marsh birds, and wading birds. Golet subscribed to the principle that in general, as wetland size increases so does wildlife value, so wetland size was important factor for determining wildlife habitat potential in his approach. Other important

15

variables included dominant wetland class, site type (bottomland vs. upland; associated with waterbody vs. isolated), surrounding habitat type (e.g., natural vegetation vs. developed land), degree of interspersion (water vs. vegetation), wetland juxtaposition (proximity to other wetlands), and water chemistry.

For this analysis, wetlands important to waterfowl and waterbirds are identified in a separate assessment (see above) and rare wetlands are addressed in the function called "conservation of biodiversity" (see following subsection). Emphasis for assessing "other wildlife" was placed on conditions that would likely provide significant habitat for other vertebrate wildlife (mainly herps, interior forest birds, and mammals). Opportunistic species that are highly adaptable to fragmented landscapes are not among the target organisms, since there seems to be more than ample habitat for these species now and in the future. Rather, animals whose populations may decline as wetland habitats become fragmented by development are of key concern. For example, breeding success of neotropical migrant birds in fragmented forests of Illinois was extremely low due to high predation rates and brood parasitism by brown-headed cowbirds (Robinson 1990). Newmark (1991) reported local extinctions of forest interior birds in Tanzania due to fragmentation of tropical forests. Fragmentation of wetlands is an important issue for wildlife managers to address. Some useful references on fragmentation relative to forest birds are Askins et al. (1987), Robbins et al. (1989), Freemark and Merriam (1986), and Freemark and Collins (1992). The latter study includes a list of area-sensitive or forest interior birds for the eastern United States. The work of Robbins et al. (1989) is particularly relevant to the Northeast as they addressed area requirements of forest birds in the Mid-Atlantic states. They found that species such as the black-throated blue warbler, cerulean warbler, Canada warbler, and black-and-white warbler required very large tracts of forest for breeding. Table 1 lists some area-sensitive birds for the region. Ground-nesters, such as veery, black-and-white warbler, worm-eating warbler, ovenbird, waterthrushes, and Kentucky warbler, are particularly sensitive to predation which may be increased in fragmented landscapes. Robbins et al. (1989) suggest a minimum forest size of 7,410 acres to retain all species of the forest-breeding avifauna in the Mid-Atlantic region.

The analysis identifies two basic wetland types with potential for providing highly significant habitat for other wildlife: 1) large wetlands ($\geq$ 20 acres) regardless of vegetative cover but excluding pine plantations, and 2) smaller diverse wetlands (10-20 acres with multiple cover types). These two categories cover most wetlands along stream corridors that connect large wetland complexes. In addition to these wetlands, large clusters of small wetlands located within a forest matrix are also recognized as having high potential for wildlife habitat as well as vegetated wetlands connected to other vegetated wetlands by forests. The remaining vegetated wetlands are designated as having moderate potential significance for providing wildlife habitat.

Please note that in general, ponds are not listed as important as significant for "other wildlife." Wildlife species living in ponds, such as several species of frogs and turtles, are mentioned in the discussion of fish and shellfish habitat, since wetlands designated as important for fish and shellfish are provide required habitat for these species.

High   Large vegetated wetlands ($\geq$20 acres, excluding open water, nonvegetated areas, and pine plantations), small

16

diverse wetlands (10-20 acres with 2 or more covertypes; excluding EM5 or open water as one of the covertypes), areas with large numbers of small isolated wetlands (within an upland forest matrix and including small ponds that may be vernal pools)

Moderate   Other vegetated wetlands

Given the general nature of this assessment of "other wildlife habitat," other individuals may want to refine this assessment in the future by having biologists designate "target species" that may be used to identify important wildlife habitats in a particular watershed. After doing this, they could identify criteria that may be used to identify potentially significant habitat for these species in the watershed. Dr. Hank Short (U.S. Fish and Wildlife Service, retired) compiled a matrix listing 332 species of wildlife and their likely occurrence in wetlands of various types in New England from ECOSEARCH models (Short et al. 1996) that he developed with Dr. Dick DeGraaf (U.S. Forest Service) and Dr. Jay Hestbeck (U.S. Fish and Wildlife Service).[6] DeGraaf and Rudis (1986) summarized habitat, natural history, and distribution of New England wildlife. Much of what is in the ECOSEARCH models comes from this source. These sources may be useful starting points for determining relationships between wildlife and wetlands.

---

[6]Copies of the matrix can be obtained by contacting R. Tiner (address on title page).

Table 1. List of some area-sensitive birds for forests of the Mid-Atlantic region. (Source: Robbins et al. 1989).

Species	Area (acres) at which probability of occurrence is reduced by 50%
Neotropical Migrants	
Acadian flycatcher	37
Blue-gray gnatcatcher	37
Veery	49
Northern parula	1,280
Black-throated blue warbler	2,500
Cerulean warbler	1,700
Black-and-white warbler	543
Worm-eating warbler	370
Ovenbird	15
Northern waterthrush	494
Louisiana waterthrush	865
Canada warbler	988
Summer tanager	99
Scarlet tanager	30
Short-distance Migrants	
Red-shouldered hawk	556
Permanent Residents	
Hairy woodpecker	17
Pileated woodpecker	408

Conservation of Biodiversity

In the context of this assessment, the term "biodiversity" is used to identify wetlands that may contribute to the preservation of an assemblage of wetlands that encompass the natural diversity of wetlands in a given watershed. Four types of wetlands may be identified: 1) certain wetland types that appear to be scarce or relatively uncommon in the watershed, 2) individual wetlands that possess several different covertypes (i.e., naturally diverse wetland complexes), 3) complexes of large wetlands, and 4) regionally unique or uncommon wetland types. The first two categories may include some wetlands that are human-impacted (e.g., impounded, excavated, timber harvested) or created; they support an uncommon wetland type and have been included as significant from our broad perspective. Some investigators may not consider such wetlands to be worth highlighting for "biodiversity" because they are the result of human actions and may not be viewed as reflecting "natural" conditions. Users can make their own decisions on how to regard these findings.

Schroeder (1996) noted that to conserve regional biodiversity, maintenance of large-area habitats for forest interior birds is essential. As mentioned previously, Robbins et al. (1989) suggest a minimum forest size of 7,410 acres to retain all species of the forest-breeding avifauna in the Mid-Atlantic region. Consequently, forested areas 7,410 acres and larger that contained contiguous palustrine forested wetlands and upland forests were designated as important for maintaining regional biodiversity of avifauna in the Mid-Atlantic Region based on recommendations by Robbins et al. (1989). This criterion will be applied throughout the Northeast as no comparable data are available for other areas of the region. A few large wetlands in a watershed (e.g., possibly important for interior nesting birds and wide-ranging wildlife in general) and wetlands that are uncommon types (based on NWI mapping classification and not on Natural Heritage Program data) may also be identified as significant for biodiversity. The size of the "large" wetlands is variable depending on the distribution of size classes in a watershed, but they should typically be larger than 100 acres. All riverine and palustrine tidal wetlands and estuarine oligohaline vegetated wetlands are identified as significant for this function because they are often possess some of the most diverse wetland plant communities in the Northeast. We also identified other specific wetland types of particular interest to biodiversity. Phragmites-dominated wetlands are generally excluded from the listing except in urban areas where large stands (e.g., New Jersey Meadowlands) are recognized as significant natural habitats.

Use of Natural Heritage Program data and GAP data have been suggested, but use of these data is beyond the scope of our remotely sensed approach to wetland functional analysis. Consequently, wetlands designated as potentially significant for biodiversity by the W-PAWF assessment are simply a starting point or a foundation to build upon. Local knowledge of significant wetlands and Natural Heritage Program data can be applied by others to further refine the list of wetlands important for this function for specific geographic areas.

The following are examples of wetlands viewed as potentially significant for the conservation of biodiversity in the Northeast:

Regionally
Significant   Estuarine oligohaline vegetated wetlands (excluding <u>Phragmites</u>-dominated)

Riverine tidal emergent wetlands (including tidal flats that are often colonized by nonpersistent plants during the growing season)

Palustrine tidal emergent wetlands (excluding <u>Phragmites</u>-dominated)

Palustrine tidal scrub-shrub wetlands

Atlantic white cedar swamps

Calcareous fens

Bald cypress swamps

Eelgrass beds

Lotic fringe wetlands

Areas with clusters of vernal pools

Headwater seep wetlands?

Rare plant habitats

Forested wetland-forested upland complexes >7410 acres in size

Locally
Significant
(possibly)   Urban wetlands

Shrub bogs

Mussel reefs

Oyster reefs

Larch swamps

Northern white cedar swamps

Hemlock swamps

Estuarine emergent wetlands (some areas)

Lentic fringe wetlands (EM/AB and AB/EM wetlands)

Uncommon types based on Inventory results

Summary

The U.S. Fish and Wildlife Service is attempting to add descriptors for landscape position, landform, and water flow path to its wetland digital database in the Northeast when updating NWI maps and digital data. When combined with typical NWI attributes from Cowardin et al. 1979 (system, subsystem, class, subclass, water regime, and special modifiers), the database contains many properties for each wetland that can be used to produce a preliminary assessment of wetland functions for large geographic areas. The focus of these analyses is on watersheds which are important land planning units for a number of agencies and organizations, but the same procedures can be applied to other land units such as counties or physiographic regions. The subject report provides the rationale for the criteria used to identify wetlands of potential significance for ten functions. These functions include: 1) surface water detention, 2) coastal storm surge detention, 3) streamflow maintenance, 4) nutrient transformation, 5) sediment and other particulate retention, 6) shoreline stabilization, 7) provision of fish and shellfish habitat, 8) provision of waterfowl and waterbird habitat, 9) provision of other wildlife habitat, and 10) conservation of biodiversity.

Acknowledgments

Many people had a hand in developing these correlations over the past five years. During this period, various iterations of these correlations were used to identify potential wetlands of significance for the specified functions in several watershed assessment studies. These studies were conducted in Maine, New York, Pennsylvania, Delaware, and Maryland. The present document reflects input from the numerous individuals including: Dan Arsenault, Matt Schweisberg, and Doug Thompson (U.S. Environmental Protection Agency, Region I), Bob Houston and Stewart Fefer (U.S. Fish & Wildlife Service, Gulf of Maine Office), Jay Clement and Christine Godfrey (U.S. Army Corps of Engineers, New England District), Jeanne Difranco, Alison Ward, and Don Witherall (Maine Department of Environmental Protection), Ken Elowe, Francis Brautigam, Sandy Eldridge, and Phil Bozenhard (Maine Department of Inland Fisheries and Wildlife), Betty McInnes (Cumberland County Soil and Water Conservation District, Maine), Katherine Goves (Casco Bay Estuary Project), Andy Cutko (Maine Natural Areas Program), Marcia Spencer-Famous (Maine Land Use Regulation Commission), Bob Bistrais (Maine Office of GIS), Wende Mahaney (U.S. Fish and Wildlife Service, Maine Field Office), Eugenie Moore and Steve Pelletier (Woodlot Alternatives), (U.S. Environmental Protection Agency, Region I), Mike Bartlett and Bill Neidermyer (U.S. Fish & Wildlife Service, New England Field Office), Jackie Sartoris and Liz Hertz (Maine State Planning Office), Dr. Jerry Longcore (U.S. Geological Survey, Biological Resources Division), Dr. Christopher Pennuto (University of Southern Maine), Dr. Hank Short (U.S. Fish & Wildlife Service, Northeast Region), Laurie Machung (New York City Department of Environmental Protection), Amy Jacobs and Mark Biddle (Delaware Department of Natural Resources and Environmental Control), David Bleil, Katheleen Freeman, Cathy Wazniak, Mitch Keiler, and Bill Jenkins (Maryland Department of Natural Resources), Julie LaBranche (Maryland Department of the Environment), Marcia Snyder, Dr. Dennis Whigham, and Dr. Don Weller (Smithsonian Environmental Research Center, Edgewater, Maryland), Dr. Matt Perry and Jon Willow (U.S. Geological Survey, Biological Resources Division), Peter Bowman (Delaware Natural Heritage Program), Nicholas Staats (U.S. Fish and Wildlife Service, Lake Champlain Fish and Wildlife Resources Office), Dr. Arthur Gold (University of Rhode Island), and George Haas (U.S. Fish & Wildlife Service, Regional Migratory Bird Coordinator). Their contributions to this effort are greatly appreciated.

References

Askins, R.A., M.J. Philbrick, and D.S. Sugeno. 1987. Relationship between the regional abundance of forest and the composition of forest bird communities. Biol. Cons. 39: 129-152.

Bowden, W.B. 1987. The biogeochemistry of nitrogen in freshwater wetlands. Biogeochemistry 4: 313-348.

Brinson, M. M. 1993a. A Hydrogeomorphic Classification for Wetlands. U.S. Army Corps of Engineers, Washington, DC. Wetlands Research Program, Technical Report WRP-DE-4.

Brinson, M.M. 1993b. Changes in the functioning of wetlands along environmental gradients. Wetlands 13; 65-74.

Buresh, R.J., M.E. Casselman, and W.H. Patrick. 1980. Nitrogen fixation in flooded soil systems, a review. Advances in Agronomy 33: 149-192.

Carter, V. 1996. Wetland hydrology, water quality, and associated functions. In: J.D. Fretwell, J.S. Williams, and P.J. Redman (compilers). National Water Summary on Wetland Resources. U.S. Geological Survey, Reston, VA. Water-Supply Paper 2425. pp. 35-48.

Cowardin, L. M., V. Carter, F. C. Golet, and E. T. LaRoe. 1979. Classification of Wetlands and Deepwater Habitats of the United States. U.S. Fish and Wildlife Service, Washington, DC. FWS/OBS-79/31.

DeGraaf, R.M. and D.D. Rudis. 1986. New England Wildlife: Habitat, Natural History, and Distribution. U.S.D.A. Forest Service, Northeastern Forest Expt. Station, Amherst, MA. Gen. Tech. Rep. NE-108.

DeLaune, R.D., R.R. Boar, C.W. Lindau, and B.A. Kleiss. 1996. Denitrification in bottomland hardwood wetland soils of the Cache River. Wetlands 16: 309-320.

Freemark, K. and B. Collins. 1992. Landscape ecology of breeding birds in temperate forest fragments. In: J.W. Hagan III and D.W. Johnston (editors). Ecology and Conservation of Neotropical Birds. Smithsonian Institution Press. pp. 443-453.

Freemark, K.E. and H.G. Merriam. 1986. Importance of area and habitat heterogenity to bird assemblages in temperate forest fragments. Biol. Cons. 36: 115-141.

Golet, F.C. 1972. Classification and Evaluation of Freshwater Wetlands as Wildlife Habitat in the Glaciated Northeast. University of Massachusetts, Amherst, MA. Ph. D. dissertation.

Hammer, D.A. 1992. Creating Freshwater Wetlands. Lewis Publishers, Inc., Chelsea, MI.

Matsuguchi, T. 1979. In: Nitrogen and Rice. International Rice Research Institute, Los Banos, Philippines. Pp. 207-222.

Mitsch, W.J. and J.G. Gosselink. 2000. Wetlands. Van Nostrand Reinhold, New York, NY.

Nelson, W.M., A.J. Gold, and P.M. Groffman. 1995. Spatial and temporal variation in groundwater nitrate removal in a riparian forest. J. Environ. Qual. 24; 691-699.

Newmark, W.D. 1991. Tropical forest fragmentation and the local extinction of understory birds in the eastern Usambara Mountains, Tanzania. Conservation Biology 5: 67-78.

Novitzki, R.P. 1979. The hydrologic characteristics of Wisconsin wetlands and their influence on floods, streamflow, and sediment. In: P.E. Greeson et al. (editors). Wetland Functions and Values: The State of Our Understanding. Amer. Water Resources Assoc., Minneapolis, MN. pp. 377-388.

Patrick, W.H., Jr. undated. Microbial reactions of nitrogen and phosphorus in wetlands. The Utrecht Plant Ecology News Report No. 11 (10): 52-63.

Patrick, W.H., Jr., and R.A. Khalid. 1974. Phosphate release and sorption by soils and sediments: effect of aerobic and anaerobic conditions. Science 186: 53-55.

Peterjohn, W.T. and D.L. Correll. 1982. Nutrient dynamics in an agricultural watershed: observations on the role of a riparian forest. Ecology 65: 1466-1475.

Robbins, C.S., D.K. Dawson, and B.A. Dowell. 1989. Habitat area requirements of breeding forest birds of the Mid-Atlantic states. Wildlife Monogr. 103: 1-34.

Robinson, S.K. 1990. Effects of Forest Fragmentation on Nesting Songbirds. Illinois Natural History Survey, Champaign, IL.

Schroeder, R.L. 1996. Wildlife Community Habitat Evaluation Using a Modified Species-Area Relationship. U.S. Army Corps of Engineers, Waterways Expt. Station, Vicksburg, MS. Wetlands Research Program Tech. Rep. WRP-DE-12.

Short, H. L., J. B. Hestbeck, and R. W. Tiner. 1996. Ecosearch: a new paradigm for evaluating the utility of wildlife habitat. In: Conservation of Faunal Diversity in Forested Landscapes. R. M. DeGraaf and R. L. Miller (editors). Chapman & Hall, London. pp. 569-594.

Simmons, R.C., A.J. Gold, and P.M. Groffman. 1992. Nitrate dynamics in riparian forests: groundwater studies. J. Environ. Qual. 21: 659-665.

Simpson, R.L., R.E. Good, R. Walker, and B.R. Frasco. 1983. The role of Delaware River freshwater tidal wetlands in the retention of nutrients and heavy metals. J. Environ. Qual. 12: 41-48.

Tiner, R.W. 1995. A landscape and landform classification for Northeast wetlands (an operational draft). U.S. Fish and Wildlife Service, Ecological Services, Northeast Region, Hadley, MA.

Tiner, R.W. 1996a. A landscape and landform classification for Northeast wetlands. U..S. Fish and Wildlife Service, National Wetlands Inventory Project, Northeast Region, Hadley, MA.

Tiner, R.W. 1996b. Keys to landscape position and landform descriptors for Northeast wetlands. U.S. Fish and Wildlife Service, Ecological Services, Northeast Region, Hadley, MA.

Tiner, R.W. 1997a. Keys to landscape position and landform descriptors fo U.S. wetlands (operational draft). U.S. Fish and Wildlife Service, National Wetlands Inventory Program, Northeast Region, Hadley, MA.

Tiner, R.W. 1997b. Piloting a more descriptive NWI. National Wetlands Newsletter 19(5): 14-16.

Tiner, R.W. 1997c. NWI Maps: What They Tell Us. National Wetlands Newsletter 19(2): 7-12. (Copy available from USFWS, ES-NWI, 300 Westgate Center Drive, Hadley, MA 01035)

Tiner, R.W. 1998. In Search of Swampland: A Wetland Sourcebook and Field Guide. Rutgers University Press, New Brunswick, NJ.

Tiner, R.W. 1999. Wetland Indicators: A Guide to Wetland Identification, Delineation, Classification, and Mapping. Lewis Publishers, CRC Press, Boca Raton, FL.

Tiner, R. W. 2000. Keys to Waterbody Type and Hydrogeomorphic-type Wetland Descriptors for U.S. Waters and Wetlands (Operational Draft). U.S. Fish and Wildlife Service, Northeast Region, Hadley, MA.

Tiner, R. W. 2002. Keys to Waterbody Type and Hydrogeomorphic-type Wetland Descriptors for U.S. Waters and Wetlands (Operational Draft). U.S. Fish and Wildlife Service, Northeast Region, Hadley, MA.

Tiner, R.W. 2003. Illustrated Keys and Mapping Codes for Application of Wetland Landscape Position, Landform, Water Flow Path, and Waterbody Type Descriptors in the United States. Draft report.

Tiner, R.W. and G. DeAlessio. 2002. Wetlands of Pennsylvania's Coastal Zone: Wetland Status, Preliminary Functional Assessment, and Recent Trends (1986-1999). U.S. Fish and Wildlife Service, National Wetlands Inventory Program, Northeast Region, Hadley, MA.

Tiner, R., S. Schaller, D. Peterson, K. Snider, K. Ruhlman, and J. Swords. 1999. Wetland Characterization Study and Preliminary Assessment of Wetland Functions for the Casco Bay Watershed, Southern Maine. U.S. Fish and Wildlife Service, Northeast Region, NWI-ES, Hadley, MA.

Tiner, R., M. Starr, H. Bergquist, and J. Swords. 2000. Watershed-based Wetland Characterization for Maryland's Nanticoke River and Coastal Bays Watersheds: A Preliminary Assessment Report. U.S. Fish and Wildlife Service, National Wetlands Inventory Program, Ecological Services, Northeast Region, Hadley, MA. (on web listed under publications at: http://wetlands.fws.gov)

Tiner, R.W., H.C. Bergquist, J.Q. Swords, and B.J. McClain. 2001. Watershed-based Wetland Characterization for Delaware's Nanticoke River Watershed: A Preliminary Assessment Report. U.S. Fish and Wildlife Service, National Wetlands Inventory Program, Ecological Services, Northeast Region, Hadley, MA.

Tiner, R.W., H.C. Bergquist, and B.J. McClain. 2002. Wetland Characterization and Preliminary Assessment of Wetland Functions for the Neversink Reservoir and Cannonsville Reservoir Basins of the New York City Water Supply Watershed. U.S. Fish and Wildlife Service, National Wetlands Inventory Program, Ecological Services, Northeast Region, Hadley, MA.

U.S. Fish and Wildlife Service. 2003. Gulf of Maine Watershed Habitat Analysis. Version 3.1. Gulf of Maine Coastal Program Office, Falmouth, MA. (http://gulfofmaine.fws.gov)

Wada, H., S. Panichsakpatana, M. Kimura, and Y. Takai. 1978. Soil Sci. Plant Nutr. 24: 357-365.

Wang, L., J. Lyons, P. Kanehl, and R.Gatti. 1997. Influences of watershed land use on habitat quality and biotic integrity of Wisconsin streams. Fisheries 22(6): 6-12.

Whigham, D.F., C. Chitterling, and B. Palmer. 1988. Impacts of freshwater wetlands on water quality: a landscape perspective. Environ. Manag. 12: 663-671.

Whiting, P.J. 1998. Bank storage and its influence on streamflow. Stream Notes July 1998. Stream Systems Technology Center, Rocky Mountain Research Station, Fort Collins, CO.

Yarbro, L.A., E.J. Kuenzler, P.J. Mulholland, and R.P. Sniffen. 1984. Effects of stream channelization on exports of nitrogen and phosphorus from North Carolina Coastal Plain watersheds. Environ. Manag. 8: 151-160.

www.ingramcontent.com/pod-product-compliance
Lightning Source LLC
Chambersburg PA
CBHW081220280526
45787CB00006B/2455